P9-CFB-499

CONSCIOUS

Books by Bob Rosen

Grounded
Leadership Journeys
The Catalyst (Jeanne Liedtka and Robert Wiltbank)
Just Enough Anxiety
Global Literacies (Patricia Digh, Marshall Singer, Carl Philips)
Leading People (with Paul Brown)
The Healthy Company (with Lisa Berger)

BOB ROSEN

New York Times Bestselling Author of *GROUNDED*

EMMA-KATE SWANN

CONSCIOUS

The Power of Awareness in Business and Life

WILEY

Published by John Wiley & Sons, Inc., Hoboken, New Jersey.
Published simultaneously in Canada.

For general information on our other products and services or for technical support, please contact our Customer Care Department within the United States at (800) 762-2974, outside the United States at (317) 572-3993 or fax (317) 572-4002.

Wiley publishes in a variety of print and electronic formats and by print-on-demand. Some material included with standard print versions of this book may not be included in e-books or in print-on-demand. If this book refers to media such as a CD or DVD that is not included in the version you purchased, you may download this material at http://booksupport.wiley.com. For more information about Wiley products, visit www.wiley.com.

Library of Congress Cataloging-in-Publication Data

Names: Rosen, Bob, 1955- author. | Swann, Emma-Kate, author.
Title: Conscious : the power of awareness in business and life / by Bob Rosen, Emma-Kate Swann.
Description: Hoboken, New Jersey : John Wiley & Sons, Inc., [2018] | Includes index. |
Identifiers: LCCN 2018015050 (print) | LCCN 2018015996 (ebook) | ISBN 9781119508441 (epub) | ISBN 9781119508465 (pdf) | ISBN 9781119508458 (cloth)
Subjects: LCSH: Leadership. | Awareness. | Organizational change.
Classification: LCC HD57.7 (ebook) | LCC HD57.7 .R6569 2018 (print) | DDC 658.4/06—dc23
LC record available at https://lccn.loc.gov/2018015050

Cover Design: Wiley
Cover Image: ©aleksandarvelasevic/iStockphoto

Printed in the United States of America
10 9 8 7 6 5 4 3 2 1

To Jay, Kaye, Robin, and Peter

Contents

PART III
THINK BIG To See a World of Possibilities

PART IV
GET REAL With Your Accelerators and Hijackers

PART V
STEP UP To Your Highest Potential

CONSCIOUS

PART I

Conscious Is the New Smart

CHAPTER 1

The Wild, Wireless World

It is not the strongest of the species that survives, nor the most intelligent. It is the one that is most adaptable to change.

—Charles Darwin

Charles Darwin's visit to the Galapagos Islands in 1835 changed biology and natural science forever. Yet almost two centuries later, the true impact of Darwin's work has yet to be fully realized. Whether we recognize it or not, change is the only reliable constant of modern life. Change is the rule. Adaptation is survival. Being conscious is how you thrive.

Let us introduce you to the chameleon, an animal that can teach us how to adapt and survive in a disruptive and accelerating world. But first we need to rethink the chameleon and start viewing it for what it is: A powerful icon of change and a world champion of adaptation.

Evolutionary forces created an incredible paradox in the chameleon. They are one of the slowest and also one of the fastest animals in nature. In spite of their sluggish-looking exterior, chameleons possess the world's fastest tongue. While commonly standing on a tree branch moving just a few centimeters an hour, a chameleon's tongue springs upon its prey with astonishing swiftness. If a chameleon's tongue were a race car, it would travel from zero to 60 mph in 1/100th of a second. This speed and intensity exists almost nowhere else in the terrestrial world.

Chameleons also developed fully independent eyes, giving them a 360-degree arc of visibility around their bodies. Able to see in visible and ultraviolet light, their eyes have the highest power of magnification of any vertebrate. These adaptations were all essential to the chameleon's survival and growth.[1]

Yet chameleons are most well-known for their ability to change color. Their base color is camouflage, enabling them to ambush their prey as they sway in the breeze. But that's just one of their colors. In fact, changing color is an adaptation that allows the chameleon to stand out and communicate with other chameleons. Brighter colors normally indicate aggression and darker colors indicate submission. They are essentially living mood rings.[2]

Now, most of us don't want to be called a chameleon. To us that signifies devious, manipulative, or dishonest behavior. Yet, as science reveals the truth about the chameleon, it's time we become more conscious of the chameleon's true place in the world. Comfortable in its own skin. Always showing its true colors. Seeing in all directions. The chameleon teaches us what it takes to adapt and thrive in a constantly changing world.

We humans are not easily intimidated by the chameleon. In fact, we are the most advanced species on the planet. What distinguishes us from all the other species is our amazing brain. Weighing in at three pounds and large for our size, the human brain is a complex network of billions of nerve cells with trillions of connections with our bodies and the outside world. The human mind, as we like to call it, is the seat of our complex thought, the source of our language, the originator of our personality, and the home of our emotions. Our capacity to be conscious – to be aware of ourselves and our surroundings – is what makes us the talk of the animal kingdom.

Yet, as humans, we find ourselves living at a critical inflexion point in our history. Everything is changing around us, from technology and demographics, to geopolitics and climate, to lifestyles and marriages, and the list goes on. Our challenge is that the world is changing faster than our ability to adapt.

Some of us respond to these changes like we are in a burning house, ever running to put out fires, believing we are operating in a world of scarcity. Others of us live like we are playing shuffleboard on the deck of a sinking ship, disengaged and uninterested in what's happening around us. Then there are those of us who are aware and anticipate these changes, in search of a better, more prosperous life.

Yet, many of us are unprepared for these accelerations. We act on autopilot as new challenges confront us. We are too reactive to problems and miss out on opportunities. We get hijacked by outdated ideas, misguided values, and polarizing relationships. We face uncertainty with fear and mistrust. Stress and burnout are pervasive as many of us do not perform to our highest potential. At a time when we need to think deeper, learn faster, and collaborate better, our minds, in their current form, are simply unprepared for this new reality.

Like our friend the chameleon, we must rely on our unique assets to guide us into our next phase of transformation. Only you can embrace these changes and adapt into the future. Lifting your gaze outside yourself while looking inward to remove the roots of resistance is how you become more conscious. With just enough urgency, resilience, and curiosity, you can activate your mind to adapt. This requires transforming yourself in an increasingly disruptive and accelerating world.

The path from clueless to conscious is paved with disruption. The going isn't easy; the road is littered with tiny jolts of uncertainty and occasionally buffeted by massive speed bumps of disruption. In life and business, we all are looking to move forward and contribute something of value. However, our wild, wireless world is ever changing and complex. It's far too easy to get lost and stay unaware of the disruptive forces that stand in our way. We have reached a time in history where our ability to adapt is struggling to keep pace.

NAVIGATING THE SIX DISRUPTORS

Like a wildfire, disruption is both good and bad. Wildfires can devastate as they destroy everything in their path. They can also rejuvenate fields and forests to bring forth new life. Similarly with people, disruption can throw us into a state of chaos or help us change and adapt. Let's look at the six main disruptors we experience every day.

- **Speed:** The pace of life is escalating and it doesn't appear to be slowing down any time soon. This forces us to see, think, feel, and act faster. While speed creates excitement and many new opportunities, it can easily toss us off balance. We can become overwhelmed and exhausted. We can sabotage ourselves by insisting on perfection, setting unrealistic goals, overworking our bodies, or burning out.
- **Uncertainty:** Stability is an illusion and uncertainty is reality. We want to believe that we will find comfort in the predictable, but it doesn't exist. Brexit changed the future of Europe, the stock market alters retirements daily, jobs no longer last a year, and no segment of business is immune from the power of disruption. We need to accept change as inevitable and develop the ability to navigate in a world of impermanence. But how do you stay grounded in all that unpredictability?
- **Complexity:** Complexity is part of the DNA of the modern world. But how do you navigate through all the knowledge, choices, and diversity in our lives? Our natural response is to create clarity in the face of confusion. But with massive amounts of knowledge, we quickly oversimplify complex issues and overcomplicate simple choices, both of which activate our biases and prejudices.
- **Technology:** As a powerful disruptor, technology is both our liberator and our slayer. It allows us to learn just about anything, meet anyone, do business in any market, and communicate instantaneously around the world. The downside is it's too easy to fall into the Internet's version of a black hole, pushing people to see the world through an increasingly narrow lens.

- **Competition:** As the fuel in our free market society, competition fosters innovation, strengthens talent, and improves quality. Yet, it can also turn us into islands of self-interest. History is littered with people and companies, from Lance Armstrong to Wells Fargo, all of whom fell from grace because of an overly competitive spirit. How do we find purpose and meaning in a world of powerful competitive urges?
- **Globalization:** First there were explorers, then there were shipping lanes, and then business went global. Today we are a click away from anyone in the world. We are all global citizens as money, markets, people, and communities are interconnected. How do we succeed individually while thriving as one global planet and society?

These six disruptors impact countries, companies, and communities alike. What we don't talk about is the impact they have on YOU, personally. At any moment in time, these forces can have a positive or negative effect on you, and fundamentally alter the way you live and work. Like winds of change, they occur all at once, stopping, starting, swirling, and combining to take us places we've never been before.[3]

On the bright side, embedded in every challenge is an opportunity. How you respond to these forces can be energizing and create unlimited opportunities, or they can be demoralizing and sabotage our best efforts. How conscious you are of yourself, your relationships, and your surroundings will make all the difference.

THE COST OF UNAWARE PEOPLE

Imagine biking down a street in Manhattan in a designated bike lane. Passing on the left is an endless procession of speedy cabs and limousines. On your right, you flash past hundreds of parked cars. Suddenly, a car door opens and you can't get around it, so you're forced to feel the true cost of unaware people.

Being unaware is a big liability. And it's happening more regularly in the face of these disruptors. It's someone who offends a colleague with an unwitting faux pas. Or someone who ignores a customer's concern and loses the sale. It's someone who is tone-deaf to the needs of his team. Or alienates his boss with a flippant comment. It's a parent who ignores his teenager's drug problem or a government worker who takes a small bribe. The list goes on and on. The cost of unaware people is just too high to pay these days – especially when the antidote, becoming more conscious, costs little but returns exponentially.

Let's face it. There is a growing gap between those who are awake in the world and those who are asleep. The faster the world changes, the bigger the gap becomes. Most people believe they are self-aware, but research shows that only 10 to 15% of us truly have this capability.[4] Some of us are changing and adapting with the times. Others are falling behind. There are four reasons why we are not changing fast enough:

- **Too shallow.** We don't go deep enough into our human psyche. We spend little time self-reflecting and stay stuck in negative emotions, shackled by old baggage, resulting in little understanding of ourselves. Since we don't have a clear mirror that reflects how we show up in the world, our relationships with others are often stunted. We underestimate the potential of people and ourselves.
- **Too narrow.** We live in steel bunkers and can't see our way out. We don't challenge our outdated assumptions, which limits the power of our expansive minds. Accepting a world of biased minds and limited perspectives causes us to miss opportunities, avoid diversity, and react irrationally to world affairs.
- **Too safe.** We are afraid of change and prefer to avoid the uncertainty around us. As a result, we stay stuck, biased and reactive. We don't use our natural positive accelerators to push us forward, and we trip over our negative hijackers that undermine us. By being too safe, we atrophy and fail to evolve and transform, leaving us standing in place as the world turns.
- **Too small.** If your view of yourself and the world is too small, you won't see connections, possibilities, or solutions. Staying small and never stepping up is sure to lead to regrets and will undermine

your highest potential. It takes courage to unleash your personal power and take responsibility, both of which are central to living a productive life.

Organizations are feeling the brunt of our lack of awareness. Markets are changing faster than the ability of organizations to reinvent themselves. There's a growing gap between the leaders we have and the leaders we need. Executives are being questioned about their ability to lead change in the future. The Gallup Organization reports that 70% of employees are disengaged.[5] And executives are deeply worried about the talent gap in society. As a consequence, many organizations are shackled by slow execution, lack of growth, unhealthy cultures, and underperformance.

Our communities are also not working well together. Cynicism and diminishing trust are impeding our ability to solve our most complex problems. Broken families, racial tensions, and sexual harassment coupled with trade wars, national tensions, and climate change are exacerbating the situation. This is happening at a time when people across the globe must come together to solve society's most pressing challenges – human rights, discrimination, the poverty gap, and environmental sustainability.

Our world is skidding toward a new economic and social era where the cost of unaware people is too high to pay. We need to wake up. To grasp the true meaning of being conscious, you are going to have to Go Deep and discover your inner world, Think Big to see a world of possibilities, Get Real to be more honest and intentional in leadership and life, and Step Up to your highest potential.

AT HEALTHY COMPANIES

We have spent over 30 years studying and advising executives, their teams, and organizations around the world. Our primary focus has been leadership and transformation. We go into organizations and meet leaders in their environment. We have interviewed over six hundred CEOs and thousands of executives in over 50 countries.

And we have published seven books on leadership, focusing on leading people, teams, change, growth, and globally.

What have we learned? The most effective people in the world today are transformational leaders at all levels—executives and managers, politicians and civil servants, parents and principals, coaches and entrepreneurs. They are all masters of personal and organizational transformation. They have honed their ability to learn faster, create smarter, and collaborate deeper, making them masters of adaptation. Now more than ever, being conscious is their antidote for disruption.

Conscious is our eighth book on leadership. It reveals our most important lesson yet. It is a message relevant for everyone who leads other people – which is all of us. Inside this book are ideas drawn from psychology, biology, management, leadership, neuroscience, and behavioral economics. This book is not about delving into your unconscious brain. We'll leave that to the psychoanalysts and neuroscientists. It also goes beyond emotional intelligence to examine the broader capabilities needed to survive and thrive. Mindfulness is also a hot topic today. In *Conscious,* we believe this is an important practice, but one of many required to navigate this wild, wireless world.

At Healthy Companies, we have noticed something dramatic happening. Being conscious is quickly becoming an essential tool for the best executives and managers. Organizations need everyone to adapt and transform in the changing world. Conscious people bring their best selves to the table and challenge others to redefine what it means to be successful. Choose to be the one with the headlights on, not the one driving in the dark.

HOW TO READ THIS BOOK?

Conscious is written as your personal guide through change - to help you adapt, accelerate, and transform.

The book is organized into five sections: The first section is the introduction: Conscious Is the New Smart. This section lays out the overall context of the book and introduces you to a few essential ideas that will help you understand why conscious is so critical today and tomorrow. The main part of the book is designed around the four sections that follow: Go Deep, Think Big, Get Real and Step Up. Here you will find specific lessons to help you become more conscious. Along the way, you will meet individuals from all walks of life around the world who exhibit many of the qualities of being conscious. Practical tips and advice are sprinkled throughout the book.

We believe each of you will approach the book in your own way. Some of you will read from cover to cover. Others will pick out chapters that reflect your own interests. Still others will use it as a catalyst as you deal with specific problems. You might want to ask yourself a few overriding questions as you read. How prepared am I for the changing world around me? Where are my strengths, my blind spots, and areas for improvement? How well am I practicing the lessons in this book? Am I emerging as a more conscious person?

On this learning journey, we suggest you open yourself up to a fresh perspective on your life. Our hope is that on completion you will have deepened the conversation with yourself, and enhanced your life and leadership skills. You will have improved your own self-awareness, your awareness of others, and your view of the world around you.

CHAPTER 2

Conscious Is the New Smart

The Devil Wears Prada is a great example where fiction depicts reality better than fact – especially when one of the best actresses of a generation shows you how to do it. Meryl Streep outdoes herself portraying Miranda Priestly, the perfectionist head of a glamorous fashion magazine in New York City. Revered in the glitzy world of international fashion, Miranda is the movie's villain. Her modus operandi is to create fear and loathing wherever she goes. Her employees describe her as a dream-crushing boss at her happiest when everyone around her is panicked, nauseous, or suicidal. Narcissistic, closed-minded, and uncaring, the Priestly Streep portrays a monument to bad leadership, unaware and asleep at the helm.[1]

The "Devil" in the film is the boss we all dread and hope to never encounter. Yet, people are drawn to the character because many aspire to reach her level of success. Streep makes Miranda believable by demonstrating real behaviors we see in daily life. Her toxic leadership is the product of a culture that encourages jockeying to be the smartest, most creative person in the room. There is no reason why Miranda had to become such a toxic leader.

Everyone has a choice on how they show up in the world. The good news is there are leaders who understand the power of being aware. Take the example of Mary Barra, chairman and CEO of General Motors Company, the first female CEO of a major global automaker. Barra rose through the ranks of GM, starting at the age of 18 as an intern. Over the years, she developed deep knowledge of GM's unique dynamics, its foibles and strengths, its people, customers, and competitors. She's worked on the factory floor, became an engineer, and eventually landed in the corner office. She unabashedly declares her love for the car business.[2]

Barra took over General Motors at a time when it was rocked by a massive safety recall. By the time it was over, nearly 30 million cars were recalled. Undeterred, she kept it honest and simple in her remarkable US Senate testimony: "The facts are the facts. We will do what is needed to make things right and we will hold ourselves fully accountable."[3]

During that testimony, Barra apologized for the recall and took responsibility to expose all of the truth. She expressed remorse and empathy toward the victims and their families. At a critical moment, Barra used the power of awareness to move GM beyond the scandal and successfully guide the company to emerge from the biggest safety crisis in its history.

The antithesis of Miranda Priestly, Barra demonstrated a leadership style that was positive and confident as she transformed the automaker's business to be competitive again in the global marketplace. So far, her impact is being felt on the company's financial performance with three years of record earnings. Mary Barra has earned widespread respect for honesty and integrity and serves as the model and champion of GM's new culture of accountability.

THE POWER OF AWARENESS

In an age of acceleration, being aware is your single most important asset. It helps you stay agile in a frenetic world. It keeps you curious as the world becomes more uncertain and complex. And it helps you stay authentic and generous as your relationships get bumpier. Remember, the world is changing faster than you are, and you must keep up. By staying aware, you create a positive impact on yourself, others, and your world.

Being aware occurs at three levels of introspection (see Figure 2.1):

- **Aware of yourself.** This refers to your own understanding about who you are – how you see, think, and feel; what motivates your actions; and how you impact other people.
- **Aware of others.** This refers to your insights about other people, what motivates them and makes them tick, and how their actions affect you and others.
- **Aware of your environment.** This refers to your understanding of life's situations and circumstances – the organizational, community, and societal forces that affect you every day.

Wait a minute! In our fast, frenzied lives, action and results are the name of the game. Not awareness and introspection. Our culture

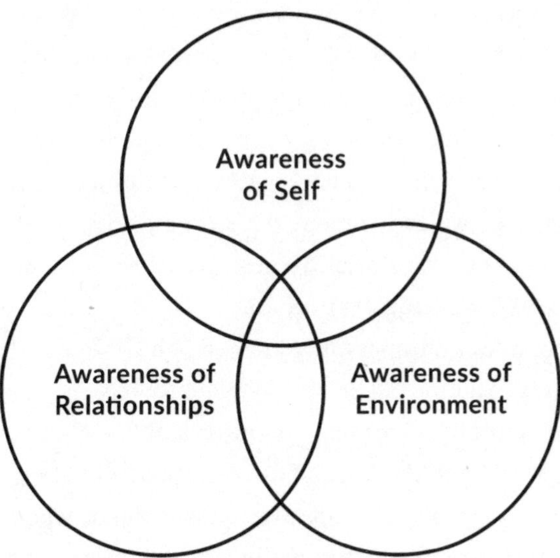

Figure 2.1 The three levels of awareness.

seduces us into thinking that the best course is to act – to chase goals, create tips, produce stuff, and make money. We believe a life of action is more valuable than a reflective one. We are constantly busy and find it hard to go deep and do the inner work of personal development. Indeed, action is often the path of least resistance. It is harder to stop, pause, and reflect from a crazy life than it is to continue to cruise unaware on autopilot.

Like an open secret, everybody knows being more aware of yourself, others, and your environment will lead to a better life. Yet, the nature of awareness is so unassuming and inconspicuous, few of us recognize its importance day-to-day.

That is why true awareness must be intentional. It cannot be purchased or inherited; it must be discovered. The result of personal initiative and effort, it lets you understand your real problems of living and helps you imagine the real solutions of what's possible in life. The power of awareness lets you transcend impulsive or instinctual responses and take deliberate action.

But it does not come naturally. In fact, 83% of our brain tissue is unconscious and controls 96 to 98% of our perceptions and actions.[4] That's right. We spend most of our day operating on autopilot, not knowing exactly what causes us to think or feel the way we do. We filter data and information through our perceptual filters – background, education, expertise, age, life experience, and culture. This creates unconscious biases that influence our behavior. The more awake we are, the less we struggle with our blind spots. As we increase our level of awareness, we move from seeing life in black and white to seeing life in color.

So, why does awareness matter so much these days? Doesn't it get in the way of acting efficiently? Why do we have to sit and ponder ourselves when results are what are rewarded? Simply, because this is not a zero-sum game. Action and awareness are not at war with each other. In fact, the real power of awareness is found when we master action and introspection together. This combination is at the heart of this book.

Conscious = Awareness in Action

WHY CONSCIOUS IS THE NEW SMART

Imagine you are back in the third grade. Do you remember the panels of perfect handwriting plastered at the front of the room? Everyone knew who the best scribe was. This was the beginning of our lifelong journey to become the smartest person in the room. Tests and grades came next, followed by accolades and admonishments from our parents, awards and recognition for hard work, and eventually appraisals and promotions at work.

For many of us, we still believe that being smart is the best path to success. If we could just learn a new subject, get an advanced degree, or build a better spreadsheet, we could advance ourselves in the world. But our obsession with being the smartest person in the room doesn't work anymore. It simply gets in the way of adapting to the future.

Pete Clare is the co-chief investment officer at the Carlyle Group. He is responsible for investing tens of billions of dollars annually for pensioners, foundation, and wealthy individuals. His secret: be intellectually honest and figure out what you don't know. To Clare, humility is a business skill. "The thing that amazes me the most," says Clare, "is that some of the smartest people in the world really don't make good investors. They're so smart that they have the answer to everything. Their opinion is right and everybody else is wrong."[5]

Being smart is based on the scarcity principle, where we see the world as black and white, good and bad, winners and losers. The goal is to be smarter, stronger, and better than others and to avoid feelings of weakness and vulnerability. Driven by the need to be right, those obsessed with being smart tend to hoard knowledge, externalize blame, and mismanage relationships and risks. This sabotages our ability to thrive in a constantly changing world.

The "smart" way of thinking is guided by three fundamental principles:

- **"There is not enough to go around."** There are not enough resources, opportunities, and ideas to go around. This thinking pushes smart people to make sure they are not left out and get what is "rightfully" theirs. *"If I show them I'm the smartest person in the room, then I'll get access to a bigger share of the budget, people, and resources."*
- **"I am what I know."** Expertise fallacy is strongly in play with smart, unaware people. They value themselves based on their expertise rather than who they are as a person. "I am what I know" is a closed system where feedback threatens identity and self-esteem. They believe that knowledge comes from inside themselves, *"When you challenge my idea, you challenge me as a person."*
- **"I must rely on myself to survive."** Because there are winners and losers, to be smart is to be strong and self-sufficient. To not have all the answers is to be weak. When you have this mentality, you don't ask for help, show your vulnerability, or collaborate well with others. *"I must rely on myself to succeed in the world."*

Today, being smart is table stakes. All you need to do is look to places like Hyderabad, Seoul, Bangalore, or Shanghai, where universities are churning out thousands of tech savants and extremely qualified talent every year. But smart is not enough. So, why is there such a scarcity of awareness in the world when there is such an abundance of smart? Well we've worked hard at getting smart. Now we need to work on getting more conscious.

In this age of acceleration, we need a new approach to living and leading. Being conscious is the new smart. Nothing is more important than being aware of ourselves and our surroundings. By knowing who you are and staying committed to developing yourself, you can develop the confidence and bearing to effectively navigate in uncertain times.

Being conscious is a fresh way of living based on the principle of abundance, where we all can succeed if we learn how to adapt to change. We embrace uncertainty as a normal part of life and work. We create space for introspection. We seek feedback, share knowledge, and search for multiple right answers. We take responsibility for our development and performance. We learn to be comfortable being uncomfortable, and use that vulnerability to stay awake in the wild, wireless world.

The conscious way of thinking is guided by three fundamental principles:

- **"There is enough to go around."** This is based on the principle of openness and abundance. There is enough for everyone. Sharing trumps hoarding, cooperation trumps heroics, and generosity trumps self-interest.
- **"I am who I am."** Who I am is more impressive than what I know. I am comfortable in my own skin, so it's important to show my whole self. Humility is a strength, and asking questions is not a weakness. I feel safe being vulnerable with others.
- **"I rely on myself and others to thrive."** There is a recognition that we are not as smart as we think we are. Learning and collaboration with the environment make me stronger, more creative, and higher performing. Love trumps fear and my networks are part of who I am.

To move from smart to conscious, we need a totally different kind of development. Rather than a simple software upgrade, we need to refresh our entire mental operating system.

IT'S OUR HUMAN NATURE

Conscious distinguishes us as human beings. This way of being gives us the capacity to reflect on ourselves and tap into our mental, emotional, and spiritual states of mind. By getting to know ourselves and experiencing the fullness of life, our conscious mind helps us open up to a world of possibilities. But we must take off our mask to unveil our true self.

This essential nature is grounded in love. Lying deep inside us, we have a natural desire for humanity, a fundamental goodness as human beings, that taps into our best human nature. This is our source of pride, health, well-being, and connection.

No doubt fear is always lurking inside our survival instincts. It is just one of the dark emotions we feel every day. Greed, anger, cynicism, and selfishness show their ugly heads from time to time. This is only natural as we navigate the ups and downs of life. But if we are true to our essential nature, love will always win out over fear.

That is why conscious is a journey of choices. We have the capacity to wake up and live consciously – to see ourselves clearly, think with an open mind, feel positive emotions, and act constructively with others. Indeed, we have a choice every day to be joyous, curious, hopeful, and productive. But this takes courage.

Yet, like water flowing down a path, it is only natural for us to take the easy way out. Oftentimes that means clinging to stability or running away from discomfort and hardship. Yet being conscious looks at reality for what it is, not what we hope it to be. It lives in the present moment, not in the past or the future. And it pierces through our facades and makes friends with the good and bad, our strengths and vulnerabilities, and our celebrations and disappointments.

Conscious unleashes our full potential as human beings. By expanding our minds, enriching our experiences, and shaping our destinies, we discover our purpose in life. Being conscious enables us to approach life as a journey. Equipped with everything we need – an open mind and heart, confidence and resilience, and our capacity for greater consciousness – we embrace the uncertainty of life. Conscious is the accelerator for effective change. The more conscious we are, the faster we adapt, and the higher performing we become.

The obsession with being the smartest person in the room doesn't work anymore. It simply gets in the way of adapting to the future. We have put too much faith in the cult of smart at the expense of ourselves, our organizations, and our communities. We must now take ourselves to the next level of development and performance.

CHAPTER 3

The Path to Being Conscious

Aviation is the safest form of transportation. Yet there is something uncertain each time a plane takes off. Wind gusts, passengers, pilots, and weather are just a few of Mother Nature's manifestations. To best manage these uncertainties, the plane is designed with maximum flex. It is intentionally built to adjust, adapt, and bend.

It's not a coincidence that the Wright Brothers originally built bicycles.[1] While a tricycle is designed to be steady and prevent a fall, it is inherently limited, slow, and hard to maneuver. As children, we quickly grew out of our tricycle and wanted a bike. Remember the feeling the first time you mounted a two-wheeler? It seemed illogical that you could stay upright. It was unstable and unsteady without a helping hand or training wheels.

The brothers built their first airplane understanding this. Ever since that time, all aircraft designers and engineers have required that a plane be designed with "give" – that it not be rigid or inflexible. The more rigid, the less safe, effective, and efficient. This became the standard for reliable and secure air travel.

Today's fighter jets, like the F-16, will fall out of the sky like a brick if the pilot doesn't have computer stabilization. Yet it is the design's flexibility that allows it to respond so superbly in combat. The more anchored you are, the harder it is to turn quickly in a dynamic situation. Today, all airplanes, even commercial airliners, are built to be flexible. This is clearly an advantage in the air.[2] It's also an advantage in life.

So, what can we learn from this perspective? Stability is an illusion. Uncertainty is the inherent nature of the universe. In fact, the idea of stability is a human construct we created to help us feel safe and secure in life and business. Many people long for and strive to find perfect stability or permanence. Yet, this is very limiting and keeps us stuck, slow to adapt, and risk averse, undermining our overall agility.

Sure, we want to live a steady and balanced life, and we certainly want the plane to be safe and secure in the air. But that misses the point. Both are fluctuating all the time. So, if we don't develop our conscious minds to embrace this uncertainty, we will never adapt to a disruptive and accelerating world.

THRIVING IN THE UNKNOWN

If you embraced uncertainty and decided to live a life that was intentionally agile, what would it look like? First, you'd accept that everything is changing, evolving and devolving. You would neither be predictable, nor expect the world to be. You would also accept that transformation is what we do all the time.

In Merriam-Webster's dictionary, transformation is defined as a "dramatic change in form, a kind of metamorphosis."[3] But transformation is not as big or scary as you may think. Every moment of every day, you are transforming yourself, whether you know it or not.

Take the human body, for example. Your 50 to 70 trillion cells are dying and replacing themselves constantly. Your brain cells regenerate when you sleep, your skin cells every two months. In fact, every part of the human body has its own distinct life cycle. You literally are becoming a new you all the time.[4] So, remind yourself that you are a creature built for change and growth. And it's not just you that is changing. Everything around you is changing, too.

Now, the thought of never knowing what's next may sound like a nightmare. Even knowing that there are no guarantees in life, we continually default to thinking and acting as rational agents. We calculate what will benefit us or what will cause us harm, and we act accordingly. And we believe that with the right knowledge, we can predict the future. This is where it all goes wrong.

Being smart is an illusion. Cognitive scientists Steven Sloman and Philip Fernbach, authors of *The Knowledge Illusion,* make a powerful argument. "The human mind is both genius and pathetic, brilliant and idiotic. Individual knowledge is remarkably shallow, only scratching the surface of the true complexity of the world."[5]

We can't predict a heart attack, a presidential election, or the winner of the World Series with any great certainty. Yet we still try. Why? We want a sense of stability and confidence that we are controlling our future. Yet, believe it or not, the most successful forecasters of the future are not Mensa members; they are normal people who are very conscious. They have cultivated the ability to not fall prey to bias, and they change their minds when they are given new information.

CHANGE IS MESSY AND COMPLICATED

Think of change as a seesaw. We approach and avoid it at the same time. Our survival brains protect us from uncertainty and danger. Our conscious minds look for the next opportunity. Now, for many of us, our fear of the unknown is stronger than our desire to change. That makes our view of the world generally fixed, while the external world is constantly changing. This fact makes our minds and the environment out of sync. This is not a good thing. We must surrender our current self – to take risks, embrace new challenges, think in new ways, and become comfortable with change.

One of the main reasons we get stuck is that we get trapped in our own philosophy about change. Our genetics, psychology, and experience help us develop certain beliefs about two aspects of change: One, our belief in how much personal power we have to

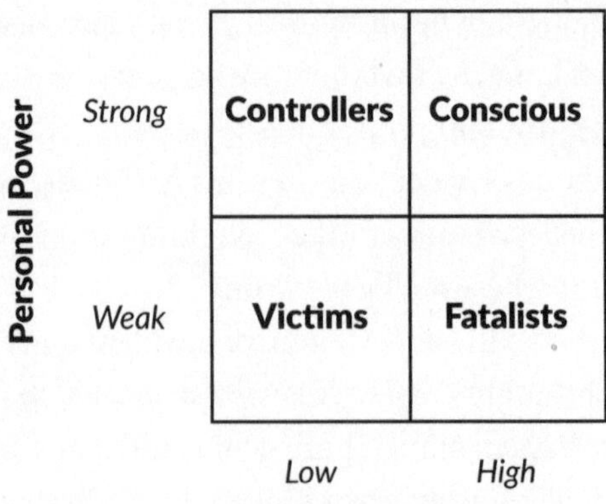

Figure 3.1 The four philosophies of change.

shape our own destiny. And two, the level of comfort we have about the uncertainty of life.

Here's the dilemma – we must get the balance between our personal power and our comfort with uncertainty just right or we succumb to becoming a victim, a controller, or a fatalist (see Figure 3.1). Let us explain.

- **Victims** – *Weak personal power and low comfort with uncertainty*

  Victims believe they have little control over their lives. Life is predictably negative, and people and the world disappoint them. They live life blaming others.
- **Controllers** – *Strong personal power and low comfort with uncertainty*

  Controllers believe they can control their lives. Things don't change much, and if they do, controllers think they can predict and control the outcomes. They live life dominating others.
- **Fatalists** – *Low personal power and high comfort with uncertainty*

  Fatalists believe life is beyond their control. Everything changes constantly, and nobody can predict the future. They live life tossed around by uncertainty.

- **Conscious people** – *Strong personal power and high comfort with uncertainty*

  Conscious people accept what they can and cannot control. They believe the world is constantly changing and people can shape their own destinies. They take pride in influencing others and respecting the mystery of life.

Being a victim, controller, or fatalist limits your capacity to adapt to a changing world. It keeps you too shallow, too narrow, too safe, and too small. In contrast, conscious people stay awake and aware of their own personal power while accepting the uncertainty of life. By living in an evolved conscious state, you can travel into the unknown, keep the bigger picture in mind, and recognize the natural impermanence of life.

Most importantly, conscious people focus on the present moment because the past is gone and the future is not here yet. With this change philosophy in mind, we have the power to transform ourselves and accelerate our potential and performance. But there are some important points to remember.

Transformation is personal. Change affects you and everyone else differently, depending on where you sit, your genetics and psychology, and how you view uncertainty and your personal power.

Transformation can be positive or negative. The Chinese character for "change" is made of two parts – "crisis" and "opportunity." The dual nature of the character reflects the reality of transformation. It can either be desirable and liberating or scary and demoralizing.

Transformation also has many faces. Some of us naturally love change and embrace the thrill and opportunity in it. Others naturally resist change and view it as disquieting and disruptive.

Whatever the case, the power to transform lies dormant inside you. We must activate that power to adapt faster in the future. It's our job to make change work for us, rather than let change happen to us. Hopeful and optimistic, courageous and resilient, and open to change – these are just a few of the attitudes and behaviors that can power up adaptation. We refer to them as your accelerators of change.

We also exhibit behaviors and attitudes that slow down our adaptation. We call these hijackers, like unconscious bias, cynicism, thinking errors, or fixed mind-sets. To accelerate our transformation, we must leverage our accelerators and minimize our hijackers. Once again, this requires a conscious mind.

THE PATH TO CONSCIOUS

Here's the new road map to guide you through uncertainty and change – to help you adapt, transform, and accelerate into the future; to prepare you for the changing times; to expand your potential and performance. Our research has found that the most successful people and leaders practice these four steps (refer to Figure 3.2).

- ***Go Deep* – Harnessing the power of introspection.** In this section, you'll learn how to get to know who you are, where you come from, and why you act the way you do. You'll tap into your innate wisdom, explore how to open your mind and heart, and get comfortable being uncomfortable. By letting go of old baggage, you will learn to be more grounded. "Go Deep" is the antidote to being too shallow.
- ***Think Big* – Getting curious and adaptive.** Think big to find a world of possibilities. In this section, you will explore how to deal with complexity and paradox. You'll also develop a curious, expansive mind; learn how to leverage your relationships and networks; and overcome unconscious biases to be a more inclusive and innovative person. "Think Big" is the antidote to being too narrow.
- ***Get Real* – Being honest and intentional.** Get real about your accelerators and hijackers. It is the best way to become more honest and intentional in leadership and life. It helps you overcome the pitfalls of being too safe and cautious. You'll learn to embrace reality and free yourself to be something bigger and better tomorrow. "Get Real" is the antidote to being too safe.

- ***Step Up*** **– Acting boldly and responsibly.** Step up to your highest potential. Here, you will learn what a conscious leader looks like – how to champion your higher purpose, stretch people in constructive ways, and be generous in your relationships. You'll also coach and mentor others, build a shared consciousness on your team, and start to build your legacy. "Step Up" is the antidote to being too small.

LESS CONSCIOUS ➡	MORE CONSCIOUS
Shallow *Unaware & Superficial*	**Go Deep** *Aware & Introspective*
Narrow *Biased & Closed-minded*	**Think Big** *Curious & Adaptive*
Safe *Protective & Reactive*	**Get Real** *Authentic & Intentional*
Small *Cautious & Self-centered*	**Step Up** *Bold & Responsible*

Figure 3.2 The path to conscious.

The rest of the book is organized in these four steps. Each step requires awareness and action. What distinguishes the people you will meet is their capacity for change. The more conscious you are, the faster you adapt, and the more effective you will be. The Path to Conscious starts with you.

LEADING IS FOR EVERYONE

Now more than ever, we need leaders to address the realities of our time. People who can Go Deep, Think Big, Get Real, and Step Up.

Who can tap their full potential, unleash the human capabilities inside their organizations, and help solve our most pressing global problems.

Whether you work at Boeing or Apple, the federal government or the state of Utah, whether you run a technology start-up or a non-profit serving the homeless, or work as the head of your household, the ability to lead change is the most important skill you must develop. Sometimes change comes from a burning platform, like cost-cutting pressures, loss of a major customer, or a problem adolescent. Other times it comes from a red-hot opportunity, such as the launch of a successful product, walking into a new job, or crafting a new sermon. Regardless of the context or the reason for the change, leaders at all levels must lead people into the unknown and into the future.

To operate in the new human economy, we need leaders from all walks of life. As we move from being preoccupied with tangible assets (land, labor, capital) to deploying the power of intangible ones (people, relationships, networks), it's people who are fluent in the language of the human experience that will make all the difference.

Why is this so important? Because success depends on tapping the hearts and minds of people at all levels of society. Today we have more knowledge and power at our fingertips than ever before. The Internet is available to nearly everyone, technology is the great equalizer, and our relationships provide the greatest advantage in business and life. How we inspire and energize others is at the heart of being successful.

So, what is leadership these days? First of all, it is not a status. Forget about all the paraphernalia of the high and mighty, from scepters and crowns to limousines and corner offices. Just as clothes do not make the man, status does not make a leader. Trappings intimidate people – which is good if you want to be a dictator or run a personality cult, but bad if you want to create an open, vibrant, high-performing family, team, company, or community.

Leading is an action, a verb instead of a noun, a relationship rather than a position. What it does is enable a group of people to pursue a shared vision and create extraordinary results. Leaders are made, not born. Leading is not some mysterious charisma that you either have or you don't. It is more like a language: We all have the capacity to learn. With awareness and experience, virtually everyone can learn to lead people consciously.

Becoming a conscious leader is a lifelong adventure. Some of us mature into leadership smoothly, while others bleed into it through crisis. But leaders are always made in real time – through experience at work and in life. Most of us have teachable moments in our lives, moments when we leapt to a new level of understanding.

For many of us, one of those moments was when we realized that we are not heroes or villains. Yet that's how so many of us think about leaders. We love them or hate them, idolize or demonize them. But humanizing is a tricky task. We expect both too much and too little from ourselves. As humans, we are learning to lead as we go, and we need to give ourselves permission to make mistakes and learn from each other.

Yet, as we humanize, we must hold ourselves to new and higher standards. We must be honest and tell the truth. We must share power and information. We must speak candidly, listen carefully, and walk our talk. Our personalities get magnified and projected onto our families, organizations, and communities. So we must work to be more aware of our inner lives.

Perhaps the most difficult, we must be humble and willing to make mistakes, to say we don't know, to express our feelings, and to ask for help. Most importantly, we must be conscious – aware of ourselves, others, and our surroundings.

Over the past 20 years, we've spent billions of dollars educating our leaders at all levels of society to prepare us for transformational change. Unfortunately, many of us – in business, government, the military, religion, sports, and politics – are not changing fast enough. Some are too self-absorbed and self-interested. Others are too complacent or overwhelmed. Others have lost their moral compass. Still others don't think they are leaders in the first place. The bottom line: There is a gap between the leaders we have and the leaders we need.

Frankly, the scorecard is quite mixed. Indeed, there are leaders and organizations who have invested in being conscious, and they are reaping the benefits. However, for many others, we have an internalization problem. Our leadership models only penetrate skin deep and ignore the whole person. As a result, our leadership development approaches have often been too tentative, resulting in inconsistent, unsustainable, and unpredictable performance. Some people dismiss these efforts as irrelevant to business, too soft when measured against financial metrics. Others are running so fast they don't take the time to learn what may be the most important leadership skill of all.

We must do a better job. First and foremost, we need leaders who are conscious people.

CHAPTER 4

Your Return on Investment

There is nothing more exhilarating than sitting in the stands as sports history is being made. While these moments rarely happen in any sport, we've seen it happen in baseball's World Series two years in a row. In 2016, the Chicago Cubs broke their infamous 108-year drought, and in 2017, the Houston Astros finally took home a pennant to Texas. Baseball fans were ecstatic. After years of data-driven fandom, heart had made a welcome return to baseball.

Ever since the Moneyball revolution of 2002 replaced intuition and experience with data analytics, the heart side of the game was seen as old-fashioned and irrelevant. Baseball became a much colder and more clinical game. Traditional pillars of the sport, like stealing bases and playing the field, became less important and were replaced by the quest for higher batting averages. Franchises became brokers of individual players rather than builders of teams. This change had profound effects on the fans and left management wondering why ratings were slumping.

Enter Theo Epstein, president of baseball operations for the Chicago Cubs. He was hired away from the Boston Red Sox for his leadership prowess, particularly his ability to develop both talent and character in his team. He understood there was value in the passion of the players as well as in the numbers. Epstein's mission was to transform the Cubs into a World Series champion. It took him four years.

Epstein's own words say it best: "I feel like I've pushed our organization back to the human being... [E]very year I just developed a greater appreciation for how much the human element matters, and how much more you can achieve as a team when you have players who care about winning, care about each other. It creates an environment where the sum is greater than the parts."[1]

Bringing home the trophy was nowhere in the cards for the Houston Astros. In 2013, the team switched to the American League and suffered the worst losing season in their franchise history (51–111). At rock bottom, they began to rebuild with newer and younger leadership. A.J. Hinch was named manager in 2014. The *Washington Post* described him as the prototype of the modern manager, "the kind sweeping the game now – young, warm, smart, approachable, open to new ideas and free of the sort of ego and experience that might make a more old-school manager bristle. Hinch is the conduit between the Astros' brain and its heart."[2]

Two months after Hurricane Harvey left Houston reeling in its wake, Hinch and the Astros came home with the World Series trophy. It was the first championship in the franchise's history – and it remains a testament to the value of playing the game with heart, on top of the numbers.

Like the Chicago Cubs the year before, the Astros demonstrated the return on investment of being more conscious. In the same way being smart is not enough in life, numbers alone are not enough in baseball. Analytics are here to stay, but the soul of baseball lies in the fans, the players, and their hometowns.

YOUR ROI IS BIGGER THAN YOU THINK

What is your return on being more aware of yourself, other people, and your surroundings? In business, return on investment, or ROI, refers to the efficiency of an investment, such as a marketing decision, a financial investment, the impact of relocating offices, or the migration to a new computer system. In life and business, ROI refers to the ability to raise your game.

If you take the time to pause and apply the approaches to becoming more conscious outlined in this book, you will experience a significant return on your investment. The personal case for making this investment of time can be as dramatic as your literal survival. Our lives are moving faster and getting more complicated every day. As a result, it is increasingly difficult to feel fulfilled, productive, and stress-free. To keep pace, we must grow more conscious.

Using your conscious mind as an asset is a new way to stand out from the crowd. Conscious people are physically healthier, happier and more fulfilled, more likely to reach their potential, and higher performers. Living in constant uncertainty may be challenging, but with a conscious mind, the return is huge.

The business case for investing in being conscious is not to be left behind. The world is changing faster than our ability to transform ourselves and organizations. Companies need conscious people to lead them into the future. The difference between a good organization and a great one is human execution and performance. Whether you are a global powerhouse or a small volunteer nonprofit, being conscious can be the true driver of success.

Trust in our institutions is at an all-time low. In business, government, media, and politics, cynicism has ripped through the fabric of our society, causing a significant loss of faith in our leaders. Whether it's the proliferation of fake news, sexual harassment, discrimination, or leaving the less fortunate behind, the health of our society is feeling the pain.

Fortunately, there are conscious leaders stepping up and recognizing that business needs to see them do the right thing. For instance, Laurence Fink, founder of the investment firm BlackRock, is rocking the boat. When the CEO of the firm controlling $6 trillion in investments speaks, people listen. "Society is demanding that companies, both public and private, serve a social purpose...

[T]o prosper over time, every company must not only deliver financial performance, but also show how it makes a positive contribution to society." This is not an idle threat. It is Fink's intention to remove his investment firm's support from companies that live only for profits and neglect to contribute to society.[3]

But it's not just companies that must step up. Government officials, religious and entertainment leaders, and everyday citizens must play their part. If we want strong communities, we need conscious and accountable people. Building a healthy community is not a spectator sport. Society wins when more people are conscious.

Finally, this book is about you. We wrote it as a guide to personal transformation. It's an opportunity to put a mirror up to yourself, take a pause in your busy life, and reflect on who you are and who you want to be in the future. Each of us has unlimited potential to transform ourselves, our families, our organizations, and our communities. But we must be deliberately conscious about it. Only then will we bring our best selves to the table, and challenge others to redefine what it means to be successful. The journey starts with you.

PART II

GO DEEP
To Discover Your Inner Self

There's a lot to see at the Kentucky Derby: Beautiful million-dollar horses, seersucker suits, and glamorous over-the-top women's hats. Unfortunately, it's ironic that the Derby participants, the main attraction, often have their vision intentionally blocked so they cannot see their surroundings.

In 2013, a favorite race horse, Palace Malice, broke from the gate and roared down the field in one of the fastest ever Derby half-miles, only to dramatically fall behind and finish in 12th place. Five weeks later, Palace Malice found himself draped in carnations standing in the winner's circle at the Belmont Stakes. The difference? No blinders (or, as they say in horse racing – "no blinkers"). At the Belmont, the colt could see the entire field – his jockey, his fellow competitors, and the thousands of roaring fans. He paced himself and won the day.

Blinkers are used to prevent horses from seeing anything that would distract or panic them. In our fast-paced world, we blinker (or blind) ourselves as well, and forfeit our greater awareness. Palace Malice's trainer thought that by blinding him with blinkers, he was doing the colt a favor by narrowing his field of vision and making him unaware. What he was doing, however, was stunting his potential.[1]

The purpose of Going Deep is to take off your blinkers and eliminate what is holding you back. What's in it for you? Being more aware of yourself and others. Living up to your potential. Coping with the speed and uncertainty of change. Turning knowledge into wisdom. These are just a few of the benefits you accrue when you work to become more conscious. Today, no one would ever know who might have been the winner of the Kentucky Derby that day. By going deep and leaving your blinders behind, you can actually increase the odds of winning in your next race.

In case you're worried, Going Deep doesn't have to involve months and months on a therapist's couch. It's something everyone can do. But, to be honest, you need to get ready to work. Going Deep is one of the most fundamental parts of becoming a more conscious person. The payoff is a healthier, happier, and more productive life. You will make better decisions, your relationships will be more positive, and your business will be higher performing.

Now here is the interesting catch. Some of the smartest people can also be some of the least conscious. Being smart does not always require you to fully know yourself. You can be a genius and neglect personal growth. Or you can know your technical craft and miss the forest for the trees. But when you stay shallow and lack intuition, you will naturally fall to the back of the pack. History gives us innumerable examples of brilliant people who were blind to themselves. Smart is simply insufficient.

People's biggest blind spots can be found in their own mirror. Their mirror is full of smudges – unclear perceptions, fixed mind-sets, negative feelings, and destructive behavior. These make us more vulnerable in business and life. Only by opening your mind can you see yourself more clearly, confront the dangers of disruption, and take advantage of the opportunities that lie ahead.

How do you know when your mirror is dirty and your mind is closed? Just by admitting to yourself about the reality of life: "We don't know what we don't know." Sounds obvious, but it's amazing how many of us live with unconscious incompetence. Boxed-in thinking, a win-lose mentality, unconscious biases, and a shallow, ethnocentric view of the world blind us from seeing the truth. And we end up living with and acting out negative emotions, like fear, anger, mistrust, or greed, which inevitably hijack our best selves.

A deeper mind expands our awareness in life. It helps us see ourselves and other people more clearly. We can free ourselves from being stuck in a cage of self-delusion. It enables us to be more broad-minded and less shackled by outdated assumptions about the world. Going deeper helps us access more positive emotions, by living with more hope, empathy, trust, and generosity. It also helps us to make deeper connections with others and frees us to embrace new ideas and solve even bigger challenges. This path to an open mind and open heart helps us to become more conscious.

You need to go deep every day. Awareness is the key to your self-discovery. In the "Go Deep" section, we're going to delve into your mind and help you accelerate your consciousness: to discover your innate wisdom, unearth your strengths and vulnerabilities, and tap into your roots of conscious living. This is the first step toward becoming a grounded and conscious person.

CHAPTER 5

Who Is That Person in the Mirror?

"Mirror, mirror, on the wall, who is the fairest of them all?" In *Snow White*, Grimm's famous fairy tale, the Magic Mirror never lies – much to the Queen's great displeasure. But in life, there's no such thing as a magic mirror. Our mirrors don't always tell the truth.

When we look at ourselves in the mirror and reflect on who we are, some of us only see what we don't want to see: Imperfections, insecurities, and weaknesses. Others of us look into the glass and only see our idealized versions of ourselves: Filled with wisdom, beauty, and morality. Neither perspective takes you to the whole truth. If all you see are flaws, you'll fail to see the potential in yourself. If all you see is good, you'll never be able improve yourself. For your whole story to emerge, you need to look deep into the mirror and become self-aware.

Has a mirror ever lied to you? Have you ever woken up, brushed your teeth, and the person staring back at you had different-colored hair or was 20 pounds thinner? Of course not. But have you ever diligently stared into your rearview mirror and cautiously backed into a telephone pole? Probably. Mirrors have a strange way of confusing us just when we really need to find the truth about ourselves. So a bit of humility will serve us well here.

In the fast, disruptive world, it is too easy to lose our center and become vulnerable to the accelerations around us. If we don't know what is core within us, we are easily blown around by the winds of change. Harry Kraemer, investor, award-winning business school professor, and ex-CEO of Baxter International, says it best: "My style of leadership starts with self-reflection. In my opinion 99% of us are just racing around and in constant motion, and don't really take the time to think."[1] The key is to get centered, to get to know ourselves, and to accept who we are trying to be.

To discover your real self, it's important to take a 360 approach to self-awareness: To look at yourself, others, and your surroundings. Personal awareness is a deep appreciation of yourself – who you are and who you aspire to be. What are your aspirations, your values, and your purpose?

Awareness of others allows you to tune in to other people: To discover what they need, what motivates them, their fears and frustrations, and how they feel about you. You might be surprised what you learn when you put yourself in other people's shoes.

Becoming aware of your surroundings is a widening view of your world. What are the challenges and opportunities around you? How does your team or organization influence you? How do your physical and social environments challenge and energize you? Mastering these aspects of self-awareness is instrumental in becoming your more conscious self. Let's get started and learn how you become who you are.

CHOOSING WHO YOU WANT TO BE

Life is like a poker game. In poker, you're dealt certain cards and then have a choice: You can hold on to what you've got or trade in your less desirable cards for new ones. Each option has potential risks and rewards. Sometimes you win; sometimes you lose. In life, you're born with certain genes and into a specific family. As you get older, you have choices: You can hold on to the person you have become or trade in your less desirable attributes for new ones. You can choose your life experiences; they also choose you. Sometimes you succeed; sometimes you fail. You are playing the game of life with four major "cards" in your hand: your genetic makeup, personal development, life experiences, and personality.

People are like Rubik's Cubes. There are more than seven billion combinations. Every one of us wants to solve our own puzzle. Yet, think about this: When did you first start to self-reflect, to focus on being self-aware? Chances are it was a random occurrence because it is rare that we were taught about the importance of self-awareness. Yet today, self-awareness is the major reason why so many of us succeed while so many others fail.

Our Genetics

Our genes give us the raw materials from which our experiences are built. We are so curious about our genetic history for one primary reason – we want to understand our hidden foundation. Since the 1990s, there has been a rapid commercialization of DNA research, fostering an explosion of interest in genetic ancestry. Today it is easy to trace your family line back thousands of years.

The Human Genome Project is one study worth mentioning. The 13-year effort was initiated to identify all the estimated 25 000 human genes and to sequence the estimated three billion pairs of genes that make up human DNA. This gargantuan task presented a remarkable finding: 99.9% of the DNA sequences were identical across the human population. This means that people everywhere are very similar, but not identical. They differ in who they are and how they live and experience their lives.[2]

Some of us are blessed with great genetic gifts and some of us are burdened with great genetic problems. Genes determine your physical vulnerability to stress and diseases. They also define how our nervous system operates. For example, DNA establishes a "set point" for anxiety and stress – whether you naturally tend to be highly sensitive or hearty and resilient. We call this "neurological diversity." These are fixed variables and are fundamental to how you become you. Living with your genetic makeup is mandatory. Letting it define you entirely is your choice.

Child and Family Development

Our childhood and family development create memories and early relationships that shape our growing identities. Most of our experiences during this time are unconscious, yet they become deep messages imprinted in our young brains. These messages impact our evolving ideas and perceptions of who we are.

Our early attachments and childhood experiences form our hidden foundation. We learn how to solve problems, relate to others, and develop a moral sense of right and wrong. We also learn about the extent of our personal power, and the inevitable impact of uncertainty when we don't get what we want. During these formative years, we develop our need to protect ourselves, and the need to learn and grow. Our childhood is peppered with conscious insight and unconscious lessons that become embedded into our personality. They usually become the attitudes and behaviors that guide us through life unless we consciously challenge and change them.

As children and teenagers, we develop the capacity for healthy relationships based on our early interactions with caregivers and friends. Unless our parents were evolved, conscious people, chances are we picked up some bad habits. You may know the phrase: "A dysfunctional family is a redundancy." Like our genetics, our child and family experiences are ever-present. When we become more conscious, this allows us to put our experiences into context. For example, "My father did the best he could in raising me" or "Parental pressure drove me to be the best" or "Conflict with my childhood friends prepared me for conflict with my husband." The more aware we are of our past, the less hijacked we become in the future.

Life Experiences

Our lives are defined by our experiences. This unique footprint of moments influences who we become. As we age and develop, we hopefully gain more control over how life's events influence us. The trick is to accept that life is unpredictable and transitory. We set out on a path, thinking we know where we are going. Along the way, we encounter obstacles, take detours, and may change direction. On this journey, we have positive and negative experiences. What matters is the lens we use to explain this journey to ourselves.

In a fast-paced world of diverse people, ideas, and marketplaces, more change creates more experiences with more opportunities, and more challenges. It's how we deal with these ups and downs that makes all the difference. Some research indicates we live with an "optimism bias" – a belief that the future will be better than the past, which gives us the tendency to overestimate positive events and underestimate the possibility that bad events will happen. And there is a small minority of people who live with "negativity bias." They see the world with the cup half empty. Researchers say these so-called pessimists actually see the world more accurately.[3]

Whether you're an optimist or pessimist, we still need to stay centered when confronting unpredictable life events. It is too easy to lose our center, too easy to be hijacked by our emotional triggers. The way to stay in control is to consciously recognize these hijackers – those behaviors and reactions that serve as triggers within ourselves. Knowing our stressors, the things that knock us down, empowers us to mitigate life's challenges. That's why it is so important to be conscious and understand that you have a choice between getting overwhelmed or using these experiences as wonderful learning opportunities.

Our Personalities

As aspiring adults, we begin to solidify our personalities. Our deep-seated beliefs and feelings become self-fulfilling prophesies. They influence how we interpret and experience life and business. We then become hardwired – psychologically and physiologically – to believe this narrative. Psychologists call this "sense making": It is our own story-creating process where we create chapters about who we are, our childhood upbringing, school and friends, and career aspirations and stories about the causes and circumstances of our life events.[4]

Our stories are works in process, like our own evolving autobiography. They influence our self-esteem, personal power, ethics and integrity, and relationships with others. By learning about our strengths and vulnerabilities, and knowing what we like and don't like, we grow into our personalities. It's important to remember that stories are created to understand our lives, and they can be rewritten to improve our lives. People are different; we have different starting points, and we have different work to do. To deepen our self-awareness, we must first understand our story.

Each one of us develops a combination of personality traits. During our early years, we grow into our unique selves. We learn about moral judgment and how to suppress and regulate selfishness. Our values begin to emerge. Studies even indicate that success among top executives is most strongly linked to moral traits such as honesty and integrity.

As we enter the cruel, crazy world, it doesn't take long, if we are lucky, to learn about what it will take to be successful to be our best selves. We immediately bump into three needs that are essential for getting ahead in life: Our need for security, our need for acceptance, and our need for control. How these needs are met – or unmet – will define our personalities and dictate our health, happiness, and success.

The **need for security** is about feeling safe and protected in the world. Without it, we feel a deep sense of vulnerability. Some of us grew up in a secure home. Others will enter adulthood more insecure. If your needs for security are not met, you are likely to act out by protecting yourself. Needing to be right, detaching from others, being overly critical, or becoming self-sufficient are a few ways we compensate. More conscious people get their security from inside themselves.

The **need for acceptance** is based on our desire to be loved and connected to others. Without acceptance, we feel alone or rejected. Some of us are natural relationship builders. Others enter their jobs and careers with anxious attachments. If your needs for acceptance are not met, you are likely to live in other people's worlds by being overly pleasing, undermining your own power, or entertaining others to be accepted. More conscious people get their acceptance by loving themselves first.

The **need for control** is about shaping and influencing your own destiny. Without control, our greatest fear is being powerless. Those who struggle with control act out by needing to over-excel, dominate, be perfect, overachieve, or manipulate others. More conscious people shape their destiny with confidence *and* recognize the uncertainty of life.

If any of these three needs go unmet, they can be even more disruptive in our accelerated lives. There are two insights you can use to protect yourself. First, we often deny that we have unmet needs. We do this by distracting ourselves through negative behaviors like overeating, over-shopping, drug and alcohol addiction, staying busy, and the biggest addiction in the modern world – overworking. Second, what we resist will persist. Many of us resist being present with the full gamut of our emotions. Acknowledging and accepting our feelings allows us to meet our unmet needs within ourselves.

One caution as you begin your 360 approach to becoming more aware of yourself: Introspection is only effective when you approach it the right way. Dr. Tasha Eurich in the *Harvard Business Review* explains that many people reflect on the question "Why?" when trying to better understand their inner world. However, most of the reasons for what we are feeling occur outside our conscious awareness, so we invent reasons that are not true. Being overly introspective can also cause rumination leading to increased anxiety and depression. The key is to create multiple hypotheses about yourself and test them out with friends, family, and colleagues.[5]

The world is more insecure, rejecting, and uncertain than ever. Being conscious helps us navigate through these murky waters – to feel safe and good about ourselves, to stay healthy and grounded, and to survive and thrive in the world. Don't leave home without your mirror.

TIPS FOR CONSCIOUS LIVING

Conduct a 360 approach to self-awareness.

- Reflect on who you are and who you aspire to be – your values, passions, and purpose.
- Seek feedback from family, friends, and colleagues about how you are showing up in the world.
- Notice how your surroundings (challenges/opportunities/organization) are affecting you.

Diagnose your personal history.

- Accept your genetic predispositions and learn to work with them.
- How have your early family dynamics shaped how you interact with others?
- Understand the personal story you tell yourself about life and work and rewrite your story to create new possibilities.

Allow your three primary needs to work for you.

- Acknowledge the three needs security, acceptance, and control and your feelings associated with them.
- Trust these needs can be met from inside yourself rather than outside yourself.
- Notice the impact of your behavior when your needs are unmet.

CHAPTER 6

Discover Your Innate Wisdom

No friend is better than your own wise heart! Although there are many things you can rely on, no one is more reliable than yourself. Although many people can be your helper, no one should be closer to you than your own consciousness.

—Genghis Khan

If you were asked to name a leader who exemplifies innate wisdom, Genghis Khan probably wouldn't be on the top of your list. He wouldn't even make your list. However, even history's tough guys couldn't have made their marks on the world if they weren't tapped into their innate wisdom. The mythology of Genghis Khan concludes he was a ruthless, brutish figure. However, he was far more complex than that. After winning a battle and suppressing existing rulers, the khan turned from a savage conqueror into a seemingly benevolent overlord. Religious freedom, meritocracy, women's rights, education and learning, and abolishing torture were all fixtures of his empire.[1]

Leaders today can learn a lesson from the Mongol paradox of tough and tender. The CEO who fights a shareholder activist trying to steal and plunder her company. A single parent who has two jobs while raising three kids. Without real mental toughness, neither the CEO nor the single dad could survive. But toughness alone is just half of the battle. The other half is mental tenderness. Without mental tenderness, the single dad will exhaust himself and neglect to nurture himself and his family; the CEO will spend too much time fighting, alienate others, and run the company and herself into the ground. The bottom line is, whether you are the Great Khan at the head of the Golden Horde or a floor supervisor at a FedEx's in New Jersey, you must be both tough *and* tender to tap into your innate wisdom.

WHAT IS INNATE WISDOM?

Part of being human is having innate capacity, an innate wisdom. We each have a natural intelligence, a genuine sense and sensibility, a fundamental sanity. Minds are naturally curious; hearts are naturally compassionate. What stands between us and our innate wisdom is the tough, cruel world we live and work in.

There is a wellspring of wisdom in each of us. And it's up to us to find and awaken it. How do you do this? You open your heart and you open your mind. An open heart fuels the fire: It enables us to be emotionally honest, compassionate, and joyful. An open mind shines a light: It enables us to be self-aware and curious, practical and relevant. An open mind and an open heart are both expressions of the better angels of our nature – principally, love.

We don't talk about love a lot at work. Yet the dismissal and denigration of love has had major consequences. Poor engagement of people, slowed creativity and innovation, dysfunctional politics, and unhealthy people are a few examples. But we know a lot about the power of love. Studies show that the highest ranked strengths in adults are consistently kindness, fairness, honesty, judgment, gratitude, and love.[2] Perhaps most surprising, the best indicator for an effective military leader is someone who values love. Not to mention that love, gratitude, hope, and zest for life are good for your health and your happiness.

There are four ways we express love:

- **Love of purpose – devoting ourselves to a greater purpose.** We are all hungry to be part of something bigger than ourselves. A purpose gives our life greater meaning and inspires hope, passion, and a desire to give back to the world.
- **Love of accomplishment – having a desire to achieve.** Nothing seems more satisfying than working hard and completing a project that you care deeply about. While explicit rewards like money, fame, or power are great, there is something especially motivating about setting a goal for yourself, making the necessary sacrifices and compromises, meeting milestones, and experiencing that sense of personal accomplishment.
- **Love of others – showing concern and care for those in your personal ecosystem.** As social animals, we are the only species in the world that exhibits complex positive emotions, like empathy, generosity, and forgiveness. A desire for belonging and connection is our natural calling.
- **Love of yourself – showing compassion for yourself.** Love starts from inside you and emanates outward. If you don't love yourself in a fundamental way, you will feel the darts of criticism more intensely – and you will be more likely to throw darts at other people.

Love is foundational, for sure. Yet in a bumpy, accelerating world, you must also build a strong sense of self to protect against the arrows on the streets. You must learn to exercise your inner resources: Grit, self-control, willpower, and self-compassion.

Grit is the ability to persist in working toward your goals. Self-control is your capacity to regulate your emotions as you interact with change. Willpower is your ability to override thoughts and impulses that undermine you. Self-compassion is our capacity to treat ourselves with the same kindness that we show others. These qualities of mental fortitude enable us to navigate through the windstorms around us.

There is an old Japanese proverb that says, "A seed not sown cannot be harvested." You have the seed of innate wisdom lying dormant inside you. It's your job to harvest it.

BARRIERS TO FINDING YOUR INNATE WISDOM

We live in a deficit society, where many of us see problems to be solved versus opportunities to be explored. In this world, the glass is often half empty. We tell ourselves, "If only I had known better," "If only I wasn't afraid to try," "If only I had more money," "If only I was smarter." People collude by falling into the trap of deficit living and leading. This half-empty mind-set is driven by anxiety, fear, and inadequacy. The world may act that way, but we don't have to. Tapping into your innate wisdom is critical and will give you the confidence to drive yourself forward.

To discover this wisdom, you need to embrace a new way of living, your natural state of abundance. This philosophy believes that you have everything you need right now. It is driven by possibility, appreciation, and gratitude. And it creates a space to open your mind and heart, and tap into your innate wisdom.

Another obstacle that gets in the way of our innate wisdom is the pursuit of more. We are conditioned to believe that happiness is always ahead of us. We're so sidetracked by the past and future that we lose sight of our ability to discover our innate wisdom today. We must remember that what we aspire to is already present. We need to improve our present-moment awareness to appreciate what we have, be who we naturally are, and live in the present. If we can't be in the present, we will never awaken our innate wisdom.

Finally, not all change is controllable. Being conscious of this reality is critical. It helps us tap into the full wisdom inside of us. Unfortunately, we too often believe we are in control of our own destiny. Being attached to this idea can cause us a lot of pain and suffering. A commute to work or a visit to the airport are perfect examples of this principle in action. Alcoholics Anonymous says it best in the Serenity Prayer: Grant me the serenity to accept the things I cannot change, the courage to change the things I can, and the wisdom to know the difference.

Uncertainty is reality in the new economy. We can help to shape our futures, but we can't always control the outcomes.

ACTIVATE YOUR INNATE WISDOM

Our innate wisdom is based on a simple dilemma – live in love or live in fear. You choose each moment of every day. With an open mind and heart, you can be naturally authentic, joyful, forgiving, and grateful. With a closed mind and heart, you can be cynical, deceitful, envious, and greedy.

Your innate wisdom also comes in handy in difficult times. When times are tough, is there a little voice inside that gnaws at you? We start deep, anxious conversations with ourselves, asking, What have we done wrong? What happens if this doesn't change? What could I have done better? Am I less than other people? Am I letting people down? Don't beat yourself up; be gentle with yourself.

When you face inevitable losses, unmet hopes, slow opportunities, or rejections, do you run and hide? This is the moment when we must reach deep inside and appreciate all that we have and use it as encouragement to stay the course.

When times get tough, is your tendency to dig moats and go into protection mode? Are you guilty of wearing helmets and armor? Do you look for scapegoats and hideouts when it gets bumpy? This is the exact opposite behavior you need to cultivate. Next time you find yourself battening down the hatches, inspire yourself to get back into the game – this time with more courage, confidence, willpower, and wisdom.

Trusting your innate wisdom needs to be practiced. As Genghis Khan recommends, "No one should be closer to you than your own consciousness."[3]

A TRIUMPH OVER FEAR

Spring comes late to the mountains of Argentine wine country. By mid-October, the Malbec grapes of Mendoza Province begin to flower on their way to bottling in April. Yet thousands of feet above, the warm South American winds of October never reach into the deep glaciers and mountain passes. Nighttime temperatures in the Andes can reach as low as 30 degrees below zero. Life there is impossible. All that exists is ice, rock, and snow. It was into this utter desolation that the 23-year-old rugby player Nando Parrado was, quite literally, thrown.

On the 13th of October, 1972, a commuter plane carrying 45 passengers crashed high up in the Andes mountains. Nando survived the crash, but his mother didn't. Three days later, his sister died in his arms. The survivors were on the mountain for 72 more days with no food and no winter clothing. Yet through superhuman perseverance, Nando and another survivor managed to climb away from the crash site and walked for 10 days back to civilization to bring help back.

It was through this profound experience that Nando learned to manifest his innate wisdom: "I was lucky enough to find out at a very early age what the important things in life are." After the plane crash, Nando says he experienced a revitalization in his life. His time on "the glacier of tears" gave him a powerful understanding of the importance of love and life. Nando lost all fear of trivial everyday risks that most people agonize over, and as a result, says he feels no trepidation taking risks in business. Today he is the CEO of six successful companies.

The greatest lesson Nando teaches is it doesn't take a near-death experience to discover your innate wisdom. His advice: "Don't be afraid, live in the moment, follow your heart and never stop changing." He encourages everyone to start breaking through their trivial issues and focus on things that truly matter, like being conscious in the world.[4]

TIPS FOR CONSCIOUS LIVING

Tap into your innate wisdom.

- Do you believe at your core that you are a wise and compassionate person?
- Would people say that you are primarily motivated by love or fear?
- Is your natural way of operating to believe the cup is half full or half empty?

Cultivate alignment between your head, heart, and gut.

- Notice your thinking, feelings, intuitions, and body sensations.
- Be aware of how your thoughts, emotions, and intuitions are connected or disconnected.
- What does this tell you that could inform your actions?

Determine what you can and cannot control.

- Be aware of and accept those parts of your life you cannot control.
- Have the courage to accept and influence the things you can control.

CHAPTER 7

Can You See the Alligator in the Trees?

Our survival instincts are not our friend in the new economy. They keep us stuck in negative emotions and slow us down in business and life. Conscious people override these fears by using their executive brain to navigate the murky waters of uncertainty.

The Everglades don't give up their secrets easily. In the 1600s, pirates used Florida's mangrove swamps as sanctuaries from the British. During Prohibition, Al Capone is suspected of having a factory deep in the Everglades to bootleg liquor. However, the lifestyle and habits of the Everglade's most iconic resident, the alligator, are well known to scientists. Or at least, we thought they were well known.

For centuries, scientists believed that the ability to climb trees was a trait extinct in today's crocodiles and alligators. When researchers went into the field to study these creatures, they looked in two places: Down into the water and at the water's edge. Despite two to three hundred years of biological study, thousands and thousands of scientific papers, and husbanding the animals in captivity, no one questioned one belief, that alligators could not climb trees. That is, until 2014, when a research team from the University of Tennessee went into the Everglades and found crocodiles and alligators in trees, day and night, pretty much everywhere they looked.[1]

So, why were scientists so unaware, so unconscious of the facts? Biases and fears probably ruled their minds. This might explain why scientists were looking down at the water while alligators were sliding onto tree limbs above them. In hindsight, it's hard to believe the scientists could have been so blinded for so long. But in many ways, it makes a lot of sense, given how the human brain has evolved. We expect the world to be a pretty scary place and we use the reptilian part of our brain to protect us. The problem lies in our failure to recognize how our reptilian brain influences and controls our thoughts and actions.

OUR THREE BRAINS

There are three parts of the human brain – the reptilian brain, the emotional brain, and the mammalian brain. We acquired each at different stages in our evolution. It's important you understand this because all three brains are interconnected and influence your thinking, emotions, and decisions.

The reptilian brain, the oldest and most primitive of the three, controls the body's vital functions such as heart rate, breathing, body temperature, and balance. As your protector, it has been programmed to detect danger for many thousands of years. It holds hardwired memories of our survival do's and don'ts. Primarily, the reptilian brain functions as an early warning system. Impulses generated by the reptilian brain are based in survival instinct and self-interest and live only in the present moment. It cannot think beyond the obvious. The roots of fear, fighting, and fleeing from danger reside in the reptilian brain. Like an alligator climbing into the treetops of your executive brain, it can easily override your rationality, hijacking your emotions and perceptions.

The emotional brain was next in evolution. The main structures of the emotional brain are the hippocampus (memories), the amygdala (emotions), and the hypothalamus (hormones). This brain controls our feelings. Negative emotions like anger, anxiety, and sadness as well as our positive emotions such as compassion, love, hope, and generosity reside here. Hardwired deep in the middle of our brain, these feelings allow us to experience and express a full gamut of emotions.

Your neocortex, the most advanced part of our brain, is home to your mammalian, executive brain. It is the gateway to consciousness. This area is involved in complex, cognitive thinking and the expression of personality. The roots of human language, abstract thought, imagination, and rationality live in this part of the brain. The executive brain allows you to see past the obvious and integrate the past, present, and future in your judgments. This advanced, distinctly human brain is all about intellect.[2] It's important to remember—The human brain and mind work interchangeably. Our brain runs on electricity and chemicals. Our mind is motored by perceptions, thoughts, and feelings. They are constantly transforming themselves all the time. The brain can change the mind and the mind can change the brain.

WHEN THE ALLIGATOR ATTACKS

Whether you know it or not, your primitive reptilian brain is a powerful player in your daily life. It can shut down and override your emotional and executive brains, and it does it more than you think. Being more conscious about where your thoughts, feelings, and actions originate is the difference between controlling your mind or letting your mind control you. Do you know what part of your brain is dominant at any given time of your day?

It is not super obvious to discern when your reptilian brain takes over. Let's look at a few routine situations you may encounter during the day. A great example of this is when you tell a meaningless lie.

For instance, if your partner asks, "Have you paid the mortgage?" and the truth is you haven't but intend to do it later, your first impulse may be to say "Yes, I sent it." It's easier to tell the little lie than explain that you're going to do it later and possibly get into an argument.

Many people have the bad habit of telling small lies to avoid conflict and confrontation and consciously or unconsciously telling small lies to avoid a fight. This is an example of the interplay between the reptilian and executive brains. The impulse to lie is driven by your reptilian brain; the crafting of the lie is done in your executive brain. The desire to protect yourself, to avoid conflict, is a hangover of your survival instinct, albeit an irrational one.

Let's look at another situation. You have found the house of your dreams and you made an offer. The sellers' real estate agent counters your offer and tries to close the deal fast, saying, "This is a one-time offer, and it's now or never – I have other buyers lined up." This is a clever tactic of many salespeople. It is an effort to trigger your reptilian brain's reactions so you won't use your executive brain to make a more rational decision. The faster the interaction, the more likely your reptilian brain has kicked in.

Now imagine what happens in the workplace. There's that panicked feeling you get after getting an impromptu call to your boss's office or when an employee wants a private meeting with you. The first thought that pops into your head is your boss is going to fire you or your employee wants to quit. This initial thought brings on a feeling of panic coming straight from your reptilian brain, trying to warn you. The problem is evolution has programmed us to confront the threat of physical danger in the wild, not in the office. Even though she may occasionally seem like it, your boss isn't a saber-toothed tiger stalking its prey between the cubicles.

These examples of daily life illustrate how easy it is to get hijacked by your reptilian brain. All of us have our own personal alligator ready to pounce into our executive brain at any moment. The scary thing about alligators is they are unseen and hunt by ambush. Not unlike fear, they can appear in an instant and be overwhelming.

CONSCIOUS TAMES THE GATOR

In today's fast and frenetic world, we are thrashed about by deadlines, accusations, rejections, and competitors. Our reptile brain sits deep in the basement waiting to be activated. It's there to protect, but often we are betrayed by our instinctual hardwiring. Overreacting with feelings of fear is not helpful for most of the situations we confront at work, at home, or in our communities.

To evolutionary biologists, this is not surprising. Our reptilian brain has been in place much longer than our executive brain. Our instincts take precedence over our thoughts. We're not always so good at willfully turning off our instincts with our thoughts, so fear wins over thoughtfulness. The reason is our survival responses are hardwired. We can get stuck in unproductive or dysfunctional habits of mind. Your relationship with fear – and its cousin, anxiety – has a profound effect on your life. It shapes how you see yourself and others, and how others see you. It influences how you think about problems and make decisions.

We need a different approach, a new way to stop the alligator from climbing into our executive brain. Being more conscious of your irrational fears and letting them go will help you become aware of the real dangers in your life – like bad health habits, risky business behavior, or toxic relationships. We are more unconscious and less aware of our reptilian brain exactly at a time in history when we should become more conscious.

For example, Vince Roche became the CEO of $4 billion Analog Devices (ADI) in May 2013. With an Irish background and a global mindset, he learned the business through a checkerboard of positions, from product management, strategic marketing and growing emerging businesses. ADI's products link the world with analog and digital signal processing technology in a wide range of industrial, automotive, consumer and communications applications.

With Vince at the helm, it's no surprise ADIs tag line is "Ahead of What's Possible." Yet it was his conscious mind that catapulted him into the top job in a company full of expert engineers. "If we are not going deep, we are not learning, sensing, and adapting to our environment faster than our competitors, and we will become extinct as a company and a species. To move beyond out reptilian survival brain, we must become very conscious of ourselves and the world. To me, conscious is living in the present, being self-aware, and seeing into the future. That's how I keep myself awake."[3]

Our ability to rewire our brains and refresh our minds is a direct result of becoming more conscious. The story of the alligator in the trees is a perfect metaphor for how easily we can be unaware. The more aware we are of the reptiles lurking in our mind, the better able we will be to navigate through the weird, wild, and wireless world.

TIPS FOR CONSCIOUS LIVING

Understand the power of the reptilian brain inside you.

- How do you experience the feelings of fear, stress, and anxiety?
- What do you notice about situations that trigger you?
- How do you respond when you are stressed or overwhelmed?

Assess, analyze, and modulate your fears.

- Notice your early warning signs (e.g. neck/back pain, heart palpitations, headaches).
- When you experience an instantaneous flash of anxiety or fear, try to calm your body and mind. Take deep breaths.
- Allow yourself time to sit with your anxiety. If you do, the angst will pass and you will become clearer about its source.

Act consciously to strengthen your capacity under stress.

- What negative thoughts and habits are contributing to your fears?
- Use your enabling emotions (e.g. hope, empathy, faith, love) to empower you.
- Reframe the story you are telling yourself about your situation.

CHAPTER 8

Discomfort Is the New Immunization

When you feel discomfort, don't shy away from the heat. Instead, walk intentionally across the hot coals. Like physical pain, discomfort serves a critical role for alerting you to what needs to be accepted, changed, or avoided. You will be a more agile and resilient person if you make friends with the ups and downs of life.

If we told you that a machine could inoculate you from discomfort, you probably wouldn't believe us. But in 1971 in Kobe, Japan, Daisuke Inoue invented a superb psychological device that did just that. He created a machine that intentionally placed people in an uncomfortable situation with the aim of inoculating them with discomfort. The result was people became comfortable with being uncomfortable. This machine was neither a drug treatment therapy nor a sensory deprivation tank. This machine was the karaoke machine.[1]

For most people, speaking in public is the epitome of anxiety. Performing in public can be even worse. The brilliance of Inoue's karaoke machine is that it puts social anxieties in perspective. He inadvertently made a performance phobia treatment device. Singing your favorite songs, singing your heart out, knowing very well that you may not be very good, and accepting that fact, is a liberating experience. What it generates is the feeling of being your real self and lets your vulnerability shine through. Think of it as an immunization, like a flu shot for being embarrassed.

Unfortunately, there is no karaoke machine built for every form of discomfort. But if brain research teaches us anything, it's that your conscious mind puts adversity and discomfort into perspective. You are far more capable of handling discomfort than you probably believe. Humans have a real capacity to transform discomfort into positive energy and momentum for change. The more conscious you are with your discomfort, the more seamless this immunization process will be. Most important, you have the power to learn from the bumps in your work and life, and not be ruled by them.

For much of human history, great hardship was viewed as the most noble of pursuits. Hardship was considered a natural part of life. Yet in modern society, we often think the opposite. We look for the shortcut to comfort. We believe the goal of life is to be happy, the goal of work is to be number 1. Ironically, our new world of comfort and convenience is so alluring it is easy to lose sight of the value of adversity. While we chase comfort, we turn on our autopilot, ignore our negative feelings, run away from fear, and become complacent to the disruptions around us. We don't realize that adversity is our greatest teacher. What is your relationship with discomfort? Do you flinch from pain or do you lean in and use it to grow?

REFRAME DISCOMFORT

The truth is, discomfort is a catalyst for learning and change. Without discomfort, you'd have neither the motivation nor the desire to fix anything. If you see uncomfortable situations as something to be avoided, you are missing out on the opportunities to grow. If you're not growing, you get trapped in shallow and narrow points of view. When you get knocked around, you dig yourself into a deeper hole and never develop the skills to get back on your feet.

In our accelerating world, it's inevitable you will regularly face adversity. The question is whether you get back up, and how fast you rebound. Our immune system protects us from disease just like our resilience system protects us from adversity. Conscious people fall down all the time and they get up easily. Getting comfortable with vulnerability and imperfection is their natural protector. We need to reframe how we see our discomfort. To do that, we first need a deeper understanding of pain.

An ancient Buddhist parable in the Sallatha Sutra explains that pain comes in two parts.[2] The *first arrow* is the initial pain, such as a failure, rejection, loss, or a simple backache. The *second arrow* is self-inflicted pain, caused by the story we tell ourselves about the situation. We fail, then we get hit by the arrow of self-doubt. We are rejected, then we get hit by the arrow of anger or sadness. We lose someone close to us, then we get hit by the arrow of loneliness. We feel back pain, then we get hit by the fear of chronic disability. The Buddha taught that there is no relief from the first arrow. It hurts and we must accept that. It's what we do with the second arrow that matters.

Conscious people embrace discomfort by acknowledging it – by allowing negative emotions to arise, flow through you, like a wave rising and falling. If we accept the reality of the first arrow, we don't need to subject ourselves to the second arrow. Pain is part of being human; suffering is self-imposed, and interferes with our ability to adapt to change. Conscious people accept that reality and avoid the suffering of the second arrow.

FALLING IN LOVE WITH YOUR IMPERFECTIONS

One of the hardest things to do in life and business is to accept your imperfections, especially as the world turns quickly. Yet, the most inspiring among us not only accept but love their imperfections and use them as assets.

One of our favorite examples is Tim Howard, the goalie of the USA soccer team. As the World Cup record holder of 16 saves in a single match, this seasoned and experienced goalie attributes his performance to being able to manage his emotions. "I don't really get too high or too low," he claims, as he has learned to lock himself into the present moment when guarding the goal. He does not obsess over mistakes or errors. He does not look back with regrets. He just channels his competitive spirit to the challenge in front of him.

What is remarkable is that Howard copes every day with Tourette's syndrome – a neurological disorder that causes involuntary tics, which can be either verbal or physical and can be wildly distracting. Imagine trying to guard against the best soccer scorers with your head churning and your body ticking!

Diagnosed as a child, Howard's ability to overcome and deal with this condition has made him a stronger person and a stronger leader. Aside from all the championships, Howard's biggest win was falling in love with his vulnerability, and using it as a competitive advantage.[3]

What are your natural strengths? Vulnerabilities? Are you shackled by the weight of your natural shortcomings? Or are you empowered by them? We each have strengths and vulnerabilities. Sometimes we are born with them; other times we develop them through the ups and downs of life. Regardless of how we got them, our job is to face our fears and flip the script from victim to victor, turning our imperfections into assets.

LEARN THE POWER OF RESILIENCE

Resilience is learning to bend, not break – to adapt to life's challenges. At any unpredictable moment, you could be blindsided by a cyberattack, a disgruntled employee, the loss of your most valued customer, an argument with your partner. Your agility enables you to shift gears, bounce back, and move in a different direction when calamity is headed your way.

We learn about resilience from repeated exposure and trials. The more we fall down and get up, the better we are able to navigate through uncertainty. But sometimes people never get the lesson. Some interesting research says that teenagers and young adults (ages 15 to 25) who have not experienced a major crisis in their life during their early years never learn the skills of resilience, and are vulnerable to mismanaging life and career hardships, which are inevitable during middle age.

TIPS FOR CONSCIOUS LIVING

Be willing to embrace the unknown.

- Every time you breathe, the world changes. Don't delude yourself in believing that stability exists.

Distinguish between what you can and cannot control.

- The more honest you are about the difference, the less time you will waste and the less angst you will feel.

Become comfortable with being uncomfortable.

- This requires that you accept yourself as imperfect by nature. Allow yourself to fall down, put a bandage on your knee, and try walking again.

Be tough enough to be gentle with yourself.

- Especially when you feel vulnerable. Cultivate confidence and humility, even when it hurts. You've been there before, and the sun will rise once again tomorrow.

Pause, reflect, refresh, and get a good night's sleep.

- Recommit to your purpose tomorrow, and get back on the bike.

So emotional resilience is learned. The brain and body learn how to not overreact while interacting with the outside world. Repeated exposure to hard times teaches your emotions that they do not need to go into a state of fight-or-flight. Researchers say this is a key quality in learning resilience and taming the stress response system. Instead of being derailed by your reaction to stress, you can harness your mind to work for, not against you.[4]

Whether you are coping with adversity, bouncing back from setbacks, or leading through uncertainty, these experiences make you stronger. When you rise to a challenge, you reveal your hidden abilities, strengthen your capacity to suffer through setbacks, and build character. Adversity and resilience also make you more sensitive and empathetic to other people's challenges. Resilience teaches us to be confident and humble at the same time.

CHAPTER 9

Your Roots of Conscious Living

> I didn't see it then, but it turned out that getting fired from Apple was the best thing that could have ever happened to me. The heaviness of being successful was replaced by the lightness of being a beginner again, less sure about everything. It freed me to enter one of the most creative periods of my life ... It was awful tasting medicine, but I guess the patient needed it. Sometimes life hits you in the head with a brick. Don't lose faith. I'm convinced that the only thing that kept me going was that I loved what I did. You've got to find what you love.
>
> **—Steve Jobs, 2005 Stanford Commencement Address[1]**

Looking closely at yourself, tapping into your innate wisdom, being vulnerable and imperfect all help you to Go Deep. The next step is to build a healthy foundation. By planting seeds that ground yourself, you strengthen the roots that protect you from the winds of change.

We all have the internal tools available to keep our feet on the ground while striving to achieve our potential. They are our roots for conscious living: How you live (physical), how you feel (emotional), how you think (intellectual), how you interact (social), how you perform (vocational), and how you see the world (spiritual).[2] Our roots work together to nourish our mind and our heart. They help us thrive in the pressure cooker we often find ourselves in. They are truly interdependent and none can be neglected. The deeper and more widespread your roots are, the bigger and more conscious you become.

PHYSICAL ROOTS

His 6-foot-5 frame makes him an unlikely candidate for the fastest human on the planet. Yet Usain Bolt holds that title. He is the epitome of speed and physical health. He lives to run. Bolt is the rare human built for speed. Most of us aren't.

To cope with the demands of speed – to get the job done faster, to learn faster, to respond to people faster – we need to attend to our bodies. Bolt and other high-performing speed athletes excel at this because they attend to:

- **Body/mind awareness.** Understanding how your body and mind work in tandem helps you manage health risks and rebound quickly from adversity, injury, or illness.
- **Energy management.** Managing your physical and mental reserves enables you to generate positive energy and remain agile, no matter what comes your way.
- **Peak performance.** Practicing healthy habits every day boosts your ability to manage stress, enjoy work-life balance, tackle challenges head-on, and optimize your health.

Our fast-paced world is here to stay. Adapt by exploring new ways to recharge your energy – try a new physical activity or play a sport you enjoyed as a child. Research the healthy habits of your favorite athlete and select one or two habits to try out for yourself. Watch what you eat. Find a wearable device you are comfortable with and experiment with apps that monitor your body's daily performance and nudge you to manage your energy.

EMOTIONAL ROOTS

Our alligators can strike anytime, so our best defense is to grow our positive emotional roots. Uncertainty is our way of life. So we need to find a protector from the stress and a generator of positive energy. The conscious person goes deep to find the answer. Ohio Congressman Tim Ryan advises: "The best thing you could do is to live deeply and completely in the present, because you will see opportunities everywhere." How to be in the moment and avoid getting pulled to the worries of the past, present, or future? Focus on:

- **Self-awareness.** Knowing who you are at your core – your strengths and vulnerabilities, values and beliefs, fears and hopes for the future – is the foundation of a conscious person.
- **Positive emotions.** Demonstrating emotions like hope, compassion, joy, empathy, generosity, forgiveness, and love is what sets the most effective people apart from their less successful counterparts.
- **Resilience.** Having an inner reserve of energy, emotional equilibrium, and self-confidence enables you to handle life's ups and downs and remain calm and steady during continual change.

Just say *no* to the "give up" reflex. We learn to give up when we perceive or experience no control over repeated bad events. When we give up, we have little resistance to adverse situations. So things move downhill quickly. If you fall into the helpless trap, you can't perceive a setback as an opportunity. Just say "No" to helplessness.

INTELLECTUAL ROOTS

The biggest disruptor to our intellectual health is the complexity in our lives. Complexity is ever-present and far too often our first response is to hit the "ignore" button. Staying shallow and gliding along the surface may work for some things in life, but in a complex world it's simply not good enough. Imagining possibilities, seeing patterns and connections, and solving problems is how we develop our minds. We can do this by focusing on the three pillars of intellectual health:

- **Deep curiosity.** Seeking new information and embracing lifelong learning deepens your understanding of issues, unlocks your creativity, and brings clarity to your search for solutions. Curiosity may have killed the cat, but it will make you a more conscious person.
- **An adaptive mind-set.** Being flexible and open to the unexpected expands your thinking, helps you handle uncertainty and ambiguity, and allows you to course-correct in real time. Adapting to new ways of working, learning, and doing business lets you expand your mental range.
- **Paradoxical thinking.** Evaluating ideas from all angles and considering seemingly contradictory concepts enables you to grasp complexity and make well-informed decisions.

The most common reason we shut down our curiosity is that we are simply running too fast. We don't take the time out of our busy lives to be curious – to stop and take a breath, to read an article or book, to take a day off to reflect, to get a coach, or to simply ask a question rather than rush in with the answer. Instead, build a curious brain. The healthiest thing you can do for yourself is to shut the door, turn off all devices, and think without interruption, several times a week (refer to Figure 9.1).

SOCIAL ROOTS

Humans are social creatures. Our connections are like electricity that bonds us together. Interactions that are worthwhile become mutually beneficial relationships grounded in respect. Building

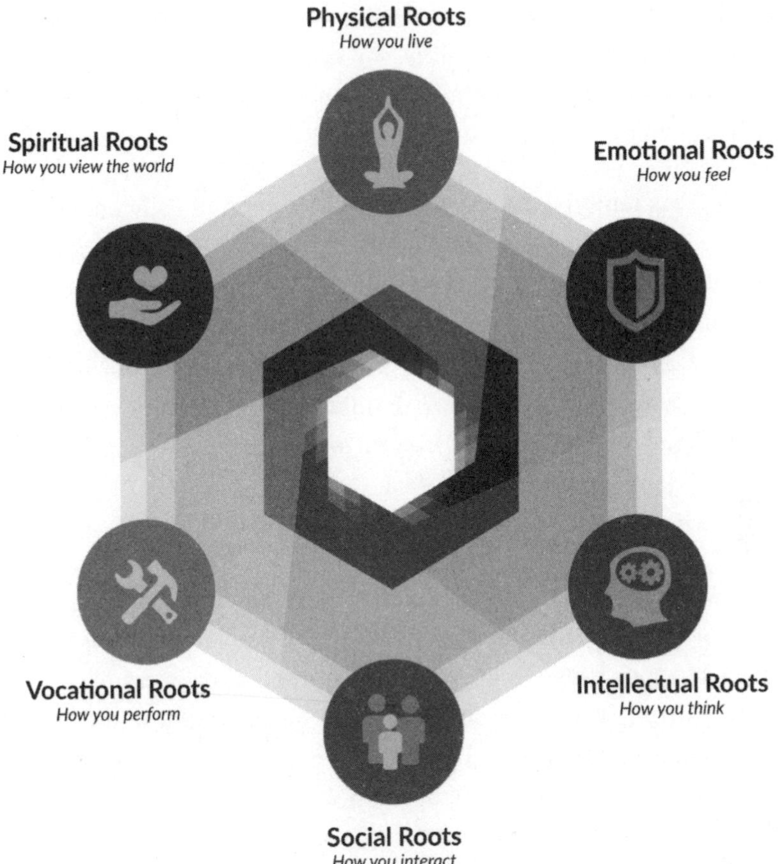

Figure 9.1 The roots of conscious living.

strong relationships requires that you understand the value you bring and how you impact others.

- **Authenticity.** Being your true self – sincere in all situations – and aligning your thoughts, words, and actions are essential ingredients in creating an environment of trust and productivity.
- **Mutually rewarding relationships.** Insisting on relationships characterized by integrity, deep listening, and honest feedback enable greater self-awareness, true partnership, and powerful results.

- **Nourishing communities.** Belonging to a group that strives toward common goals and leaves you feeling energized enriches life's experiences while forming bonds that transcend time and space.

We are rapidly adapting to the digitalization of daily life, where people and technologies are intimately connected. Being socially healthy keeps you balanced in our expanding digital world. Yet digitalization has created a new social dynamic that is not always positive. As our social networks grow, out of necessity our interactions become short and shallow. Find a good balance between deep, meaningful relationships and easy virtual ones.

VOCATIONAL ROOTS

Our world is based on competition. Careers don't crash because you are working too hard. Careers crash because you're not paying attention – to what's happening inside you, inside other people, and outside in the world. Without strong vocational health, you lose the ability to keep up. You become eclipsed by more intuitive, competent people, and your teams and organization will undermine your success. Attend to your vocational health by focusing on:

- **Meaningful calling.** Doing something that matches your values and talents gives you energy, helps you fulfill your potential, and contributes to your overall sense of well being.
- **Personal mastery.** Playing to your strengths and overcoming your weaknesses allows you to stretch yourself and perform your best. And you can model continual self-improvement for others.
- **Drive to succeed.** Having a passion for winning and knowing what success looks like enables you to achieve your goals. Even in adversity, this drive will help you navigate around, over, below, and through obstacles.

People like to live and work with successful people. So, create a Monday Morning Mantra and work on developing yourself. "I will focus on what gives meaning to me in life and work." "I will get feedback from two people this week." "I will brag about one thing I am good at this week and work on one weak spot." "I will imagine what success looks like." With good vocational health, you will inspire and engage all those around you.

SPIRITUAL ROOTS

You probably live and work with people from many different cultures. If you find yourself having "lost in translation" moments, you need to get grounded in cultural and global literacy. You don't need to necessarily travel the world to be a global thinker. But you should live with:

- **Higher purpose.** Working toward the greater good inspires you and the people around you and unleashes your most positive energy. You can become a powerful force for change and good.
- **Global connectedness.** Respecting all cultures and beliefs while being a global citizen and environmental steward helps you advance personal and business goals while making the world a better place for everyone.
- **Generosity of spirit.** Being kind with gratitude, sharing what you have, giving back to your community, and contributing to others' well-being are essential stepping stones to a happy, fulfilled life.

When you present a spirit of greater good, global connectedness, and generosity, people around you will be touched and reciprocate in kind. Spiritual health is our secret remedy for the hard-charging, self-interested world. Cultivate it one day at a time.

HIT THE "PAUSE" BUTTON

No one is a perfect six, meaning that they excel at all the roots. Some of us are on top of our physical roots and lag behind in our vocational roots. Others of us excel with intellectual roots and struggle to get control of our emotional roots. The only way to deepen our roots and stay grounded is to hit the "pause" button on a regular basis.

Make going deep your daily duty. Take deep breaths. Learn to meditate. Go for a stroll. Ponder your life's trajectory. Focus your mind on solving a problem. Feel a deep emotion. Have an uncomfortable conversation. Reflect deeply on something meaningful to you. Do something that matters every day. Make a conscious choice to pause and live a contemplative life. Show compassion and kindness to yourself and others. Make haste slowly. Then you can accelerate with purpose and action.

Steve Jobs, the late founder of Apple, used his mastery of technology and design to transform seven different industries – personal computers, animated movies, telephones, music, tablet computers, digital publishing, and retail stores. He changed the world and became a leadership icon.

Yet, Jobs was an imperfect being – just like all of us. Jobs demonstrated enormous intellectual, vocational, and spiritual health. However, his story is also a cautionary tale. He sometimes neglected his physical, social, and emotional roots, contributing to his premature death and leaving him with regrets about his personal relationships. Perfection is not a possibility, but we can strive to be our best by becoming more conscious. Sink your roots deeply into the ground and let your conscious mind be your guide.

CHAPTER 10

Travel Light

Are you stuck in the past or worrying about the future? These are one of many attachments people carry with them when they are moving too fast without being conscious. It's like dragging around a red wagon full of bricks you don't even need. These negative attachments only keep you from reaching your potential. It's just old baggage. You need to learn to travel light.

As far as anyone in the aviation industry could tell, the stars seemed to have aligned to make Ben Sliney's first day on the job picture-perfect. A low-pressure system had swept into the Atlantic and pushed Hurricane Erin out to sea. From San Francisco to Boston, there wasn't a single airport in the United States that could report any weather conditions other than "severe clear" (pilot lingo for "perfect").

Sliney's new job was as the Federal Aviation Administration's national operations manager, a position he had worked toward over the two preceding decades. He was looking forward to his first day. On a beautiful Tuesday in September 2001, Ben Sliney became responsible for all air traffic control in the United States.

Think about your first day on the job. You bring all your past experiences, good and bad, with you. If you worked in air traffic control, thinking outside of the box is the last thing you'd expect to have to do. Controllers live by rules and regulations, protocols and procedures, a right way and a wrong way to do things. If you improvise, people could die. Ben Sliney came of age in this work world.

On Sliney's first day, September 11, 2001, terrorist attacks shook the United States to its core. By 9:40 a.m., Sliney was forced to go completely off-script and respond to an unprecedented crisis. No one even knew if it was possible to immediately land almost 4,500 airplanes and 350,000 passengers safely. On top of that, Sliney had to figure out which airplanes were friends or foes, then sort through layers of bureaucracy to liaise with the military and start to protect our cities.[1]

In an incredible feat of organization and coordination, all friendly planes in the air landed safely that day. How was Sliney able to dismiss a career's worth of training and take decisive action and effectively respond so quickly? He traveled light. He accepted the uncertainty of the situation; he chose to control what he could control and trusted others; he detached himself from conventional wisdom, relied on his innate wisdom, and was willing to risk failure, thus freeing him to make the correct choices. Sliney's ability to travel light saved thousands of lives when disaster struck.

ATTACHMENTS: HOW WE POISON OUR LIVES

An elephant never forgets and a dog never remembers. Dog Whisperer Cesar Millan coaches his human clients, saying: "Being fearful in the present because of something bad that happened in the past is a human trait, not a dog trait."[2] Dogs live in the moment. They respond by visceral instinct and don't experience episodic memory. They aren't attached to emotional baggage in the way people are. The human brain is like Velcro for negative experiences and Teflon for positive experiences. This is why so many of our human attachments are poisonous.

All of us have conversations with ourselves that keep us stuck in old patterns and shackled by dysfunctional habits. Attachments come in many shapes and sizes. Some are simple thoughts and feelings. Others are more elaborate philosophies about life, desires about the future, and ideas about success. As they develop, they grow like a dense, entangled psychological web that controls our mind. We see six common human attachments at work and life: Desire for stability, clinging to the past, idealizing the future, thirsting for control, chasing success, and striving for perfection.

- **Attachment to stability.** We believe we can create stability and safety in our lives. But there is no such thing. Scared of uncertainty, we deny this reality and run away or get hijacked by change.
- **Attachment to the past.** Many of us are living in the past, trying to make sense of what's already happened, idolizing or demonizing our memories, and becoming immobilized by old emotional scars.
- **Attachment to the future.** Many of us are preoccupied and worried by the future – striving for more or better, obsessed over what is missing in our life. By fearing that something is missing in our life, we risk not enjoying the present moment.
- **Attachment to control.** From early childhood, we are taught to shape our environment. We minimize our weaknesses, maximize our strengths, and develop confidence and courage to be in charge. Then we become controlling.
- **Attachment to success.** Everyone dreams of success. But when our fear of failure or our desire for success turns into a compulsive need for achievement, then we've got a real problem.
- **Attachment to perfection.** Many of us are ruled by the need to be perfect to fill ourselves up. Perfectionism in ourselves is bad enough. But we tend to impose perfection on the people around us, and all hell breaks loose.

Peg Lorenz is ninety-two years old. She graduated from college in 1947 after the family lost everything in the depression. Married for fifty years with three sons, she became an elementary school teacher.

A volunteer her whole life, she has many interests, from travelling and theater to church and telling risqué jokes. Peg is a conscious person without a lot of attachments. Just listen to a few of her insights about life.

"To whom much is given, much is expected... You're going to die, so you might as well wake up and live life fully... The material things don't matter much. You just need to treasure the people you love... I never thought I was better than others so I don't deliberately do or say things to hurt people... It doesn't take much to make me happy. I enjoy the simple things in life... I don't have all the answers, just a lot of questions... And I don't remember things as well as I used to. But around here, nobody else does either, and we just laugh about it."[3]

Life is a journey. You can't carry everything with you all the time. On a regular basis, you need to check your bags and only carry what you need. If you don't, you let your baggage define who you are, and that's unhealthy. Learn to travel light and stop being weighed down by your emotions and attachments that get in the way.

Every morning we activate a switch when we open our eyes. We choose – consciously or unconsciously – how we want to live the day. We can choose the path of confidence, full of joy, love, curiosity, and freedom. Or we can choose the path driven by fear, littered by worry, disappointment, and suffering. The choice is ours. To overcome the emotional baggage of the toxic attachments in our lives, we need to become more conscious.

When we let go of our unhealthy attachments we can become free of suffering and sabotaging ourselves. We can trade our disappointments for joy, our worries for peace, and our fear for love.

Yet there's one attachment that seems to challenge everyone, in the United States and around the world. It's our attachment to success. Let's take a closer look.

IS SUCCESS YOUR DRUG OF CHOICE?

What does attachment to success look like? It's the people who preach at every opportunity about their accomplishments. It's neighbors who get sucked into "keeping up with the Joneses" and reach beyond their means in the cars they buy or the mortgages they take out on the houses they can't afford. It's the woman at work who can't wait to tell her colleagues about her bonus. Or the father who brags about staying late at work and misses his kid's soccer game. In each case, the image of success is driving the person's self-worth and how they present to the world.

For some, the desire for success is insatiable. Obsessed with getting ahead, these people are always raising the bar on themselves and feel jealous toward others who are successful. Others personalize the inadequacy and turn the arrows against themselves. Both types rarely relax and constantly worry about their performance.

Busy, successful people are often battling a noisy mind. Worrying about work, reliving past mistakes, or kicking yourself over a bad deal is nothing more than mental noise, and it's producing stress. It's this noise that blocks consciousness and leads to unhealthy attachments.

Driving the attachment to success is the fear of failure. Some of us simply avoid failure by leading a risk-free life. Others take lots of risks and keep plenty of balls in the air so when they do fall (as they always do from time to time), they can protect ourselves from feelings of vulnerability. Many others choose to live in their own bubble, trying to convince themselves that they are special. Some of us even have trouble giving ourselves permission to enjoy the success we do achieve. In each case, we end up living a constrained and unfulfilled life.

Everybody wants to be successful. But when our desire for success turns into a compulsive need for achievement, we've got a real problem. Suddenly we find our dreams dictating our lives. Sooner or later, we find ourselves shackled by the very success we aspire to be.

So, how do we "baggage check" a compulsive need for achievement? How do we let go of constantly wanting more, having more, being more and free ourselves from the heavy chains that keep us shackled to the treadmill of success? First, you must define yourself by who you are, not what you have. Experiences trump materials. Feel good about yourself from the inside, not by all those external trappings. Relish your recognitions. But don't depend on them. The next breath will take them away. Broaden the way you value yourself – in relation to work, personal life, family, friends, hobbies. Too much of one will make you vulnerable. Tap into your higher-order emotions – higher purpose, generosity, and empathy. Most important, go deep every day.

GO DEEP AND MOVE FORWARD

Oprah Winfrey was born into poverty to an unmarried teen mother in rural Mississippi. Sexually abused in childhood, she ran away from home at age 13 to live with her father in Nashville, Tennessee. In those early days, Oprah loved to read and found early success as a top honor student. She began college, but left at 19 to pursue a media career.

As the first female, African American news anchor, Oprah transformed *AM Chicago* from the lowest- to the highest-rated talk show in Chicago. Three years later, the show was named *The Oprah Winfrey Show*. According to CNN, the new show was one of the highest-ranking shows in American history. Yet Oprah's first boss told her she was too emotional for television. She showed him. In 1986, she founded Harpo Productions and the rest is history. Along the way she produced her own magazine, created a radio channel, and launched a cable TV network.

What distinguishes Oprah from all the rest is her unwavering authenticity. "Turning wounds into wisdom," she never let her past determine her future. Throughout the years, she let people know her deepest emotions and spoke to the vulnerability inside all of us. Says Oprah, "I had no idea that being your authentic self could make me as rich as I've become. If I had, I'd have done it a lot earlier."

As *Life* magazine's most influential woman of her generation, Oprah has become an inspirational friend to many of the world's citizens. Her messages of "listen to your gut, keep moving forward, and you are in the driver's seat" have become mantras for folks as they struggle to overcome difficult life experiences. Reflecting on her own life, Oprah shares her wisdom: "Challenges are gifts that force us to search for a new center of gravity. Don't fight them. Just find a different way to stand." Nowhere is this more apparent than in Oprah's own public struggle with her weight. By humanizing the topic, she made it safe for us to become comfortable with being imperfect.

Oprah models the principle of Going Deep. Aware of herself and others, we see her open mind and heart in action. Through her successes and struggles, we learn from her passions and vulnerabilities. We have watched her ditch the suitcases of her past and observed her pursuit of a full and conscious life. As *Forbes* magazine observes, "her momentum builds with time."[4]

Oprah's core message tells us all about the power of love over fear. Be more conscious today than you were yesterday. Check your bags, detach from the noise, and go deep every day.

TIPS FOR CONSCIOUS LIVING

- **Start a mindfulness practice.** Give yourself some private time to reflect on your life. By being present with yourself, you will heighten your awareness, reduce stress, make better connections, and improve your performance.
- **Strengthen your attention skills.** Watch how you become easily diverted by distractions. They are everywhere in today's wild wireless world. By focusing on what matters in the moment you will stay true to your intentions and get a better outcome.
- **Be aware of your attachments.** We all have our share of them. When you are feeling stressed, ask yourself, "What attachments are showing up for me? Where are they coming from? How can you reexamine and minimize them?"
- **Be mindful with others.** Listen deeply with an open mind and be fully present in your interactions. A study of 2000 leaders examining 33 leadership traits found the ability to be 'mindfully present' with others was the most important leadership skill.

PART III

THINK BIG
To See a World of Possibilities

"Imagine a world in which every single person on the planet is given free access to the sum of all human knowledge. That's what we're doing," explained Jimmy Wales. He founded Wikipedia in 2001, and it swiftly dethroned the traditional printed encyclopedia from its perch atop the family bookshelf.[1]

Wales saw the opportunity in marrying open source software and user-generated content when no one else did. Wikipedia is now ubiquitous around the world as one of the first places you look for information. Wales tapped into our thirst for knowledge and people's desire to share what they know with others. He was thinking big.

In "Go Deep," you were asked to think from the inside out, reflecting on who you are and how you want to show up in the world. In this section, "Think Big," you will be challenged to look outside yourself to see the world clearly – to expand your mind, to inspire your curiosity, and to tap into your creativity. To see the future as a world of possibility, you first need to overcome the pitfalls of being too narrow.

When you look through a peephole, your field of view is both limited and distorted. People with an unconscious bias or fixed mind-set see the world through such a narrow lens. In our complex world, many of us go on autopilot. We think too simply or get sidetracked when new challenges arise.

Learning to think big puts you in a bigger landscape. It keeps you focused on what matters. It inspires and energizes you to be something bigger. Expanding your mind is like throwing the door wide open into a world free of distortion. Everyone can think big. All it requires is opening the door of your mind.

Organizations today need people to see their work in bigger ways. To think creatively. To learn faster. To find opportunities that did not exist. To solve more complex problems. They are looking for people to take them into the future. They need everyone to rise above the din, to see the bigger picture. This requires adaptive and innovative thinking.

Isn't it ironic that the leader of an antique, conservative religion would become an icon for progressive change in the digital age? The man is none other than the leader of the Catholic Church and the bishop of Rome, Pope Francis. By using his values as his North Star and leading from the heart, Pope Francis is transforming himself as he adapts to new environments and the ever-changing demands of his job.

The very nature of the papal job is to protect the status quo with unbridled power and authority. Francis's choice of how to use that power is deeply embedded in his desire to lead for today *and* tomorrow. He promotes a global society that is more inclusive, fair, and socially responsible. He challenges us to protect the environment by warning that "the earth, our home is beginning to look more and more like an immense pile of filth."[2] And his clever use of Twitter, with 40 million followers in nine languages, has become his pulpit to evangelize and be a catalyst for positive change. The pope is thinking big.

We are living in a 280-character universe where it's easy to perceive the world as "a mile wide and an inch deep." Our personal challenge is not to get stuck in this narrow box. Whether you're a president of a pharmaceutical company, a manager in an IT department, or the entrepreneur of a start-up, you need to be curious and expansive. The first step to expanding your mind is to become your own drone, to move from the dance floor to the balcony to see over the horizon.

There are tools you can employ to think big. You can learn how to leverage your most valuable asset, your personal ecosystem. Networkers connect ideas and people to make bigger things happen. Developing a Google mind, powered by learning, is just as vital to thinking big. Like Google's search, our mind needs to continuously refresh itself. Thinking in paradoxes, under the mantra "'And' is the new 'Or,'" will show you how to abandon "either/or" thinking and replace it with a "both/and" perspective. Finally, you need to ask yourself, "Which negative biases are mine?" and act to broaden your thinking. Being inclusive is good business and the true catalyst for innovation.

CHAPTER 11

A 280-Character Universe

Put a goldfish in a fishbowl and it is unable to grow. Put a goldfish in a water garden and it can thrive as a beautiful koi for generations. Put a goldfish in a river and it will grow like mad and become an environmental pest. Put a goldfish in the ocean and it will quickly become someone else's dinner. The context of your life matters.

We are shaped by powerful forces that influence us every day. They can either blind and narrow us, like the tiny world of the fishbowl, or awaken and broaden us, like the healthy koi pond. Being aware of your environment is critical. Without a clear view of the context in which we live and work, we can easily be held hostage by its invisible forces and pressures. These forces present us with our greatest opportunities and our fiercest challenges.

Let us give you an example. In 1997, Reed Hastings was on his way to work out at the gym. He was distracted by a notice from Blockbuster saying he owed a $40 late fee. He was especially annoyed by the fact that he needed to hide the fee from his wife. That gnawing annoyance was the catalyst for a huge opportunity called Netflix.

In a few short years, Hastings's company morphed into a media powerhouse. "My greatest fear at Netflix has been that we wouldn't make the leap from success in DVDs to success in streaming," recalls Hastings. That fear was unfounded, but it gave him a broader perspective about his business. Ironically, one of his biggest failures along the path to streaming success was, once again, related to fees.

In 2011, in the rush to bring streaming to their customers, at the height of the economic recession, you might remember that Netflix raised its subscription fee by 60% and tried to spin off the DVD portion of the business. Customers were furious. Shareholders were angry, calling for Hastings's resignation. This was an a-ha moment for Hastings. He admitted loudly, "I was arrogant," acknowledged he was not listening to customers, and quickly apologized. His candor won him much praise from the public and his shareholders. Today, he is well known for being a straight shooter.[1]

You could attribute some of Hastings's early caprices to his obsession with not getting trapped in the fishbowl. His grand vision was for every Internet-connected device to be streaming Netflix videos. But Hastings needed time for the entertainment business, technology, and consumers to catch up. He kept focused on today's business, yet understood its future over the horizon.

What distinguishes Reed Hastings is his ability to understand context – "knowing what must be done now and what can be improved later." High-definition streaming was not possible in 1997, nor in 2007. By assessing changes in consumer tastes, business models, and ways of delivery and distribution, Netflix positioned itself to be at the right place at the right time, leaving competitors like Blockbusters in the dust.

Netflix transformed its business model three times in its young life to become the premier provider of streaming and content creation. In 2016, Netflix won nine Emmys with original content like *House of Cards* and *Stranger Things.* Clearly, Hastings did not get trapped in the fishbowl.[2]

So how does the story of Reed Hastings relate to your life? Are you aware of the influences and forces around you? What are the opportunities and challenges that show up on your desk? Do you think for today and tomorrow simultaneously? Do you operate with the right balance of patience and impatience in your life?

#TOOMUCHINFORMATION

Digital technology is the great human disruptor of our time. Unlimited global access to information allows anyone to learn just about anything, anywhere, at any time. You can take an online Stanford University engineering class for free at a café in Paris. You can turn to WebMD for personal health questions before going to the doctor. You can go to LegalZoom to decide if you need a lawyer. You can plan a fabulous vacation on the other side of the globe without using a travel agent. Modern digital technology has opened millions of new opportunities, shifted power dynamics and expanded globalization to a personal level.

The trouble is more and better access to knowledge is no guarantee that we can make sense of it all. Overload can be a real problem. University of Virginia researcher Timothy Wilson explains that the brain can absorb about 11 million piece of information a second but can only consciously process about 40.[3] This plethora of information can make our mind feel as if it's in a constant state of hyperventilation. Our outer world is simply changing faster than the ability of our inner world to process it all. That is why the modern learner is overwhelmed, distracted, and impatient.

In *The Shallows,* technology writer Nicolas Carr shares how the sound-bite world is rewiring our brains. Carr warns that the Internet is destroying our powers of concentration and making it difficult for us to engage with complex ideas.[4] Carr reflects on his own life, "Once I was a scuba diver in a sea of words. Now I zip along the surface like a guy on a Jet Ski." No question, efficiency and immediacy may be getting in the way of deep and broad thinking. Yet other studies are quick to point out that the Internet expands our minds and strengthens our mental muscles. Like anything, technology has its trade-offs. We'll just have to wait and see about the long-term psychological and neurological effects of the digital world. Will the knowledge overload us or enlighten us? Will technology liberate us or imprison us?

Given the hectic lives we lead, it is easy to fall into this digital trap. We go online 27 times every day. We unlock our smartphones nine times per hour and get interrupted at work every five minutes. This disruptive phenomenon is happening at a time when we need to be thinking bigger. We need to resist the easy option of falling into the Internet's version of a black hole, a click-hole where you see the world through an increasingly narrow lens. Technology allows us to reach far more people than ever before. Yet as we do that, our communications tend to become short and shallow. The result is we see and hear only things that we agree or disagree with, encouraging our biases.

CONFRONTING REALITY

There's a lot of discussion these days about "alternative facts." Too much information makes it easy to confuse the reality. Are you using fact-based assertions or opinion-based assumptions? One is verifiable; the other is not. In our fast-paced world, reality does matter.

Some people are afraid of the facts. It makes them anxious, and it's easier and less threatening to deny reality. Others avoid the facts because they don't have the answers to solve their complex problems. Still others like to live in a bubble, pretending that everything will be just fine. Their natural idealism and optimism become their Achilles heel. And then you have those who manipulate the facts by asserting alternative realities just to change the subject.

It's important to navigate through the clouds of smoke to find the facts in situations. Consider these suggestions:

- **Embrace the facts for what they are.** There is something very powerful about keeping an open mind to reality – to be clear about what's working and not working in your life.

- **Don't be impulsive with the facts.** Look the facts squarely in the eye, but don't be seduced by them. You'll find that time clarifies everything.
- **Look deep into yourself to see what keeps you from running away from the facts.** Is it your natural idealism, a tendency to spin reality, or your anxiety? The more you know about yourself, the easier it is to confront reality.
- **Talk about the facts with others.** It's amazing how often people are seeing the same problem, but viewing it differently.

Nobody said reality was easy. How you deal with reality will define your credibility. It's better to be realistic about what's in front you. Otherwise, you may trip on the facts and fall on your face.

IT'S YOUR CONSCIOUS CHOICE

We have always tended to surround ourselves with like-minded people. Digital technology reflects this phenomenon. Left on its own, our technology encourages us to stay in our fishbowl. If you choose to live too narrowly, the machine can help you. For example, marketing and advertising software tracks our online behaviors to personalize the content we see. If we mindlessly surf the Net, algorithms customized to our preferences perpetuate our unconscious biases. This dynamic contributes to polarizing people and reinforces the divisions among us.

Unless we do something different, our digital ecosystem will default to an echo chamber amplifying back at us information we already hold. This feedback loop keeps us locked in a provincial view of the world. We need to teach our computers to broaden our context and bring us information that will help us expand our minds.

Be aware that in our digital world, the pressure to be narrow and shallow is pervasive. Thinking big is the best way to navigate this ever-shrinking 280-character universe. But that is a conscious choice only you can make for yourself.

To build your own koi pond, you must become your own editor. The Internet is a big feedback loop that you can train to expand your horizon. Start editing now:

- Make a conscious decision to subscribe to both sides of an issue. Get Google Alerts for both sides of an argument.
- Read (and click on links) across disciplines, across industries, and include fiction.
- Pursue fresh ideas. Actively search for sources of information that will help you grow and develop.
- Ask others from different persuasions for alternative perspectives and suggestions.

CHAPTER 12

Be Your Own Drone

There's a new buzz over the Mille Collines ("the land of a thousand hills") of Rwanda. It's not the whispers of ethnic unrest, nor the sounds of gorillas in the jungle. It's the faint buzz of electric motors driving a drone's rotor blades. In rural Africa, it's the sound of good things to come.

Today, seven billion people inhabit the earth, nearly two billion of whom lack prompt access to essential medical supplies. Swollen rivers, political upheaval, and dirt roads are just a few of the obstructions that separate billions of rural people across the world from the medicines they need. Postpartum hemorrhaging, snake bites, and severe anemia due to malaria are a few maladies that turn deadly in the absence of prompt medical treatment. A start-up from California, Zipline, believes drone technology can solve this persistent infrastructure problem.

Rwanda is a country with 4700 km of road, yet only 1000 km are paved. There are two rainy seasons, February to April and November to January. During the wet months, travel in Rwanda is slowed to a near standstill when the roads turn from red earth tracks to impenetrable bogs. Transportation creates a unique challenge for a health care system that serves an estimated 11 million rural Rwandans. The problem is not a lack of doctors. The rains halt the resupply of blood plasma, antibiotics, HIV treatments, and medical supplies for a significant part of the year. As long as anyone can remember, millions of people in rural Rwanda simply went without during the monsoon rains.

That is, until now.

Today, a rural doctor facing an emergency can text or call a Zipline launch facility and receive what his patient needs within 20 to 30 minutes. Zipline is providing the novel solution of instant on-demand delivery of emergency supplies. They saw the opportunity to fly drones over the thousand hills of Rwanda rather than waste time going around them. "This is not a small step forward, this is a transformational change to how we provide medical care to people across the world," explains CEO Keller Rinaudo. This is thinking big.

Zipline started as a dream of a group of engineers in Silicon Valley who wanted to become a robotics company. However, they were born in the long shadows of robotics giants like Google and Amazon. Rinaudo describes the ambitious underpinnings of Zipline: "Our goal is to design airplanes as safe as Boeing but write software as fast as Facebook." Yet they needed to find a practical example for drone delivery that undeniably made sense to everyone, one that fit their business model. Where they found it was Rwanda. They also found their higher purpose as a company.[1]

GET UP ON THE BALCONY

The ability to rise above the din, to see the bigger picture, to hear the bigger story, is more important than ever in our disrupting, accelerating world. Being your own drone lets you see over the horizon. Knowing how to scan your environment allows you to see from many vantage points. With it you have greater vision, self-observation, and discovery. You can observe, hover, move forward or backward or sideways at will, developing and training your conscious mind to see connections, interdependencies, and change. You must become your own drone.

Fortunately, we have the extraordinary ability of bearing witness to our own lives. We can remember where we've been, recognize where we are, and envision where we're going. Our amazing brain can sort through, select, coordinate, and evaluate the cognitive abilities we need to do this. This thinking about thinking is called metacognition. It's like having an objective bird's-eye view of ourselves and how we are moving through our lives.

To empower yourself to think big, you need to simultaneously be an engaged participant and a wise observer. Step off the dance floor onto the balcony and become a participant observer. Metacognition allows you to see yourself and others more clearly than ever before. Think about a time in your life when you were too obsessed with yourself, when you lost perspective on what was important and risked a job, customer, or relationship. If we live without a bigger perspective, we only learn of our obvious blunders through the 20/20 vision of hindsight. If you are capable of being your own drone, rising above yourself to see the bigger picture, you won't have to learn about your mistakes through regret. Activating your drone, and thinking about your thinking, is the key to seeing emotions, events, and relationships as data that inform how you make your next move.

LAKE WOBEGON EFFECT

Every episode of National Public Radio's *Prairie Home Companion* closes with this signoff: "That's the news from Lake Wobegon, where all the women are strong, all the men are good-looking, and all the children are above average."[2]

Lake Wobegon is the fictional town in which the show is set. The show may be silly, but the Lake Wobegon effect is very serious. Social psychologists call it "illusory superiority." Humans have the tendency to overestimate their achievements and capabilities. People think their memories are better than they are. We think we are good problem solvers. And if you had to rate yourself on a scale of one to ten, you probably would give yourself a seven. And everyone else gives themselves a seven as well.

When you're up on the drone, this cognitive tendency toward optimism isn't always bad. It gives us hope and confidence about the future. But it does rose-tint our glasses. Optimism without data is just an emotion, and hope is not a strategy. When you launch your drone and look down on yourself, double-check and make sure you are not swimming in Lake Wobegon.

Remember: This cognitive bias can also play out as we move up the corporate ladder. Research shows the more power a leader has, the less self-aware he or she tends to be. In one study of over 3600 leaders, those in higher-level roles relative to those in lower-level roles were more likely to overestimate their level of skill for 19 out of 20 competencies. This included emotional self-awareness, empathy, trustworthiness, and leadership performance.[3]

Beware of the "expert effect," too. Many of us develop in our careers inductively from generalist to specialist. You start off writing code and then end up as a cyber expert. You train across like-minded companies and suddenly you are an industry expert. You go to medical school and your office sign says "pediatric oncologist." A significant pitfall is letting your mind get stuck in the expert role. The more expert we are, the less flexible we become. We get stuck in our discipline or expertise and languish in the "I am what I know" world, where being right is the most important metric. Give yourself permission to be a generalist up on the drone. It will serve you well navigating through uncertainty.

THE DAILY LIFT

Most of us struggle to see the world from our drones. Our short-term, short-sighted lives on the ground keep us from seeing at a distance. We are limited right from the start in recognizing how big our horizon really is. Our mind plays tricks on us, too. Fear of the unknown stops us from imagining the future. Too much humility undermines our confidence to take risks. Being too biased in our thinking keeps us locked in a box. All get in the way of thinking big.

TIPS FOR CONSCIOUS LIVING

Take time to reflect.

- To get up on the balcony, you need to create the space to slow down and think. What gets scheduled gets done, so schedule some time to get up on the balcony.

Look for patterns and themes that help you see connections.

- Get out of the details and look at the bigger picture – make connections in data, understand how world events relate to your life, see problems from different vantage points.

Practice being an observer and a participant at the same time.

- While in a meeting, become an observer by noticing how you are showing up –your impact on others' emotions, the quality of your listening and presence, how much talking you are doing, the impact of your body language. What are the dynamics in the group? Then join the conversation as you make real-time adjustments to your behavior.

Move constantly between the balcony and the dance floor.

- The speed of change requires you to be constantly adapting, so get on the balcony to get a new perspective, then step back on the dance floor to put the plan into action.

Understand your external environment and context.

- Getting on the balcony is about understanding your customer needs; your competition; and industry, political, technological, and social trends and how these might impact your business.

Another culprit against thinking big is the pressures from our surroundings. Organizations talk a lot these days about thinking out of the box. Yet, the reality is many workplaces are obsessed with short-term thinking and getting the work done now, which narrows our perspective and keeps our feet stuck on the ground. This may not always be a good thing.

Give yourself a daily lift. Prepare yourself for the real, diverse pressures you will face. Look outside your occupation, profession, and industry. Improve your ability to scan your environment. Test your ability to think in the present and future simultaneously. Envision possibilities by traveling into the unknown. You might be surprised how exhilarating it is to think big up on the drone.

CHAPTER 13

Leverage Your Personal Ecosystem

What's your #1 personal asset? Your skills? Your job? Your ambition? Your looks? Your mind? None of the above. Your greatest asset is your personal ecosystem. Who we know and how we connect to people in our personal ecosystems provide the strongest foundations and advantages in life and business.

To help you think big, you need to create a perpetual motion machine of ideas, energy, and relationships to achieve your goals. You can only do this with a high-functioning personal ecosystem. Our sharing economy, powered by technology, is connecting people all over the world. Those who have personal influence power to make things happen – the networkers and collaborators – are the ones who will get ahead.

As humans, we need to mirror our technology: To act fast, get connected, and think like a network. Today, what is valuable is our social currency, our earned influence. People with social currency establish trusted relationships that allow them to move faster and be more effective. How can you acquire more social currency? We suggest you leverage your personal ecosystem.

Mother Nature teaches us that everything in the physical world is connected and interdependent. A personal ecosystem is connected too, and comprises your personal brand, your positive relationships, and your networks. How these elements weave through your life creates your unique footprint.

BRAND "YOU"

Think of yourself, your reputation, as a brand, like Coca-Cola, Land's End, or Nike. Each has specific attributes and conjures up unique emotions when interacting with its customers and communities. The same is true for you.

We are all entrepreneurs, leading the brand of "You" – complete with our personal values and career aspirations, intellectual and emotional assets, and unique market differentiators. The key is to manage your career as if it were a start-up business. Like entrepreneurs, we must invest in ourselves and take our product to market.

People are sensitive social creatures. We respect those who try to connect authentically. Being yourself in public will help accomplish that. An easy smile, a quick one-liner, or a ready compliment seems automatic and natural, creating rapport and connection. But for many of us, we struggle to build confident rapport with those around us. We need to put in effort to show our genuine selves. Creating your brand "You" requires self-awareness, commitment, and humility. On the flip side, you also need to know how to brag.

There is an acceptable form of boasting. It's called "bragging rights." We give people permission to brag about real accomplishments. We often see it on social media sites, like LinkedIn. People use their "bragging rights" as a form of personal advertising. Great self-promoters understand personal marketing. It's not hubris, overconfidence, or arrogance. It's smart self-promotion. People like working with and for successful people. But it's got to be honest and real. Nobody likes somebody who is always trying to impress you or tries to deceive you.

That's why confident humility is so important. We tend to equate confidence with competence. But that is not always the case. Confident people are good at hiding their insecurities and incompetence. Their extroverted, charismatic demeanor can fool you. That's where humility comes in. It is a good reality check and when expressed publicly can be a real relationship enhancer.

When you view yourself as a brand, you're able to see opportunities to grow your personal ecosystem. It could be something as simple as finding a signature way to introduce yourself to new people. When asked, "What do you do?" you might talk about who you are. Saying, "I move people" is a thousand times more intriguing than saying, "I'm a bus driver." A short, provocative statement almost always gets the listener to explore more about you. And that's the point. The more you share about yourself and your business, the wider you can stretch your personal ecosystem.

IT'S ABOUT YOUR RELATIONSHIPS

We are biologically programmed to form social bonds and connect in deep, personal ways. No one is an island of self-interest. We are all part of the web of interconnectedness. Our mirror neurons are the intercommunicators in our brain, while our relationships are like social electricity. Your smile energizes others. Your anxiety makes people nervous. You bring the argument with your spouse at breakfast to the performance appraisal you conduct in the morning. The loss of a big client goes home with you and disrupts the family dinner.

Here's how it works: The healthier relationships are, the more information is shared. The more information is shared, the more people feel connected. The more people feel connected, the more they trust each other. The more trust people feel, the more interconnected and interdependent they will want to become. Having strong, trusted relationships with a wide range of people nourishes your personal ecosystem.

It is also important to your health. In a cover story of the *Harvard Business Review,* Dr. Vivek Murthy, US surgeon general, spoke out about the "loneliness epidemic" pervading our workplaces. It's affecting people of all ages and backgrounds and happening at a time when work has become our primary social network. Warns Murthy, "We live in the most technologically connected age in the history of civilization, yet the rates of loneliness have doubled since the 1980s."[1] Loneliness is associated with greater risk of heart disease, anxiety, and depression. It reduces performance, limits creativity, and impairs decision making. Yet if you have strong connections with people at work, your performance improves and so does your health.

There are four powerful social ingredients that can foster great relationships – empathy, fairness, communication, and appreciation.

Empathy: Don't Leave Home Without It

Empathy is deep understanding on an emotional and cognitive level about the fears, aspirations, and concerns of people. Being empathetic is not always easy. You may need to understand someone who is fundamentally different from you, confront negative feelings you have about the person, or address your fear that being too nice will send false signals. The secret is to understand what is influencing your reactions, work hard to put yourself in the other's shoes, and interact as a whole person. Don't forget to share something personal about yourself. It's amazing how good you and others will feel.

Fairness: It's Genetic and Fundamental

Human beings are intrinsically fair. Consciously or unconsciously, we monitor situations and do all we can – actively or passively – to remedy any unfairness we may witness. Conscious people fundamentally understand this unspoken principle. If you take advantage of people, they will feel it and will retaliate in one form or another. Evenhanded people generate trust and cooperation. Fair play is part of our genetic makeup. It enables us to form mutually rewarding relationships and nurturing communities.

Communication: Conscious, Clear, Courageous

Good communication is conscious: You are aware of your intentions, the situation, your psychology and theirs. Deep listening to other people, without interruption and without preparing a comeback, is a great gift you can give to others. Honest communication is clear: You know exactly what you want to communicate and you speak with clear intent. Effective communication is courageous: You are honest and straightforward yet are courageous inside yourself to let the other person own his view of the truth. His truth may be fundamentally different from your own, and fundamentally flawed. But he has the right to his truth, and it is your responsibility to listen, even if you disagree.

Appreciation: Recognition Outweighs Money

In many organizations, the absence of true appreciation is more noticeable than its presence. Studies confirm that appreciation is at least as important as money, if not more, to people. In fact, companies known for their core expressions of appreciation are 12 times more likely to show better results than companies less generous with their gratitude. At their core is respect. Everyone wants:

- Respect for my thoughts, feelings, values, and fears.
- Respect for my desire to lead and follow.
- Respect for my unique strengths and differences.
- Respect for my desire to learn and develop.
- Respect for my need to feel like a winner.
- Respect for my need to be recognized for my accomplishments.
- Respect for my personal and family life as I define it.

The most successful people are masters at building strong, diverse relationships with others as they evolve over their careers. When you personify these four attributes, you shine a light on people, expanding your personal ecosystem and the ecosystems of others.

YOUR FLOURISHING NETWORK

There is deep insight in the book *All I Really Need to Know I Learned in Kindergarten*: "Share everything and play fair." To grow your network, you really need to share – knowledge, power, and trust – and play fair.[2] Where do you learn these lessons? Naturally from our parents. Indeed, if we were lucky, our parents helped us build our first personal ecosystems.

People who consciously invest in and grow their networks stand out in the crowd. Your network could be full of family, friends, colleagues, and acquaintances. Maybe they're at church, in your country club, or on Facebook. You see them at your child's soccer match or a political fund-raiser. Look at your networks at work, school, and in your community. Ask yourself: Who are my trusted friends who give me courageous feedback? Who are the colleagues I rely on to watch my back or help me get ahead? Who are those acquaintances, ships passing in the night, who might help me with a new project? Maybe it's even your past employer. In our fast, competitive world, these networks are invaluable. They will help you develop a competitive advantage to win the best jobs and opportunities. You just need to be conscious about building the right network for you.

Great organizations are masters at building strong ecosystems, too. The best ones consciously nurture and expand their concentric circles of employees, customers, suppliers, alliances, partners, and local communities. By expanding their networks, they strengthen their influence.

Technology is the great accelerator. It powers your brand, connects your relationships, and expands your networks. With the advent of social media, you can expand your network at the tap of a key. We simply know more and have access to a widening community. It's the conscious person who will turn those networks into a powerful asset.

A PERSONAL ECOSYSTEM IN ACTION

From the Rust Belt to the Tech Belt, General Motors is a case study in transforming its ecosystem. Formerly focused primarily on physical assets, now it's all about GM's connections in the sharing economy.

GM's commitment: "Our success depends on our relationships inside and outside the company."

Nobody in the business world is more aware of the importance of the sharing economy than GM's chief talent officer, Michael Arena. His mission is to guide GM's leaders to build thousands of personal ecosystems that network together to create a collective intelligence. Arena is a firm believer that productivity, big ideas, and creative thinking happen at the intersection of people. That's Arena's secret sauce for innovation.

Arena reflects on his job: "It's all about the network and how people are connected. The meeting after the meeting is the REAL meeting these days." Michael has created GM's "Innovation Xchange Lab," an intranet of people and ideas that crisscrosses the company. It allows the best ideas and brightest minds to work collectively, rather than in silos or in direct competition with one another. Tapping into this collective intelligence is key to changing the culture within General Motors.

Here's Arena's advice to help you build your personal ecosystem:

- **Be conscious of your environment.**

  "I think it is the core of how you dance with the system. What matters is the moment in front of you right now, how present you are in the moment and how you choose to show up and not overreact or underreact to what is needed."
- **Know who your closest friends are.**

  "If I don't trust my own instincts enough to try something, I go pressure test it, and I do that with my friends. I do that with the people that I know won't lie to me and they would tell me point blank."
- **Follow the energy.**

  "Who else do I engage now? Who else would be interested in this idea, and how do I build my own internal ecosystem? Follow the energy and create an environment where an idea or concept can grow. What you're really doing is trying to manage a movement – then you can close in on the network of key influencers."

TIPS FOR CONSCIOUS LIVING

Promote your personal brand, virtually and in person.

- Communicate your passions, values, and strengths. Don't be afraid to share your real self. Stay in touch and top of mind.

Choose to share what you know.

- Don't be shy or protective about giving information away. This helps others and builds trust. The more you share, the more people will share with you.

Diagnose how you are building relationships.

- Assess yourself against the four pillars – empathy, fairness, communication, and appreciation. They will help you prevent stupid mistakes.

Go deeper with your colleagues.

- Surgeon General Murthy suggests this practice. In a weekly staff meeting, set aside five minutes to let a colleague tell a personal story about hobbies, family, dreams – something people don't know.

Get connected.

- Open your eyes. Your network is all around you. See each person as a gateway to new connections. Use technology to connect. But then meet in person to discuss shared life and business interests.

- **Dissonance is good.**

  "I'm almost as interested in the tension and disruption in the room than when I'm sensing the super buzz of agreement. I know I have struck a chord, and then you can dance to let dissonance make the idea better. You want the naysayers to test whether your idea's good enough so you can create conflict and fight for a bit. That conflict actually makes it healthier so the idea evolves and gets amplified."

At the heart of General Motors' success is technology with human sensibility. Whether it's their electric cars and self-driving vehicles or hands-free driving and zero system emissions, GM is networking and innovating into the future.[3]

CHAPTER 14

Develop Your Google Mind

Ruchi Sanghvi is comfortable getting thrown into the deep end of the pool. After graduating from Carnegie Mellon University, she joined Facebook in 2005 as its first female engineer. Later she became the product manager for the launch of Facebook's News Feed. Upon leaving Facebook, she became an entrepreneur and started a company called Cove. She subsequently sold Cove to Dropbox, then became instrumental in transforming Dropbox from a 40-engineer company to an enterprise business with over 400 engineers.[1]

South Park Commons is her next brainchild. It's a Silicon Valley learning community for mid-career technology movers and shakers. Sanghvi saw a gap in Silicon Valley for how people learn and have social impact. She wanted a place where experienced technologists (like herself) could safely learn to pivot into new ventures while staying connected to their tech community.

Everyone at the Commons is starting over. Members have achieved career success and are looking for their next big move. If someone wants to transition from infrastructure engineering to working on artificial intelligence, then this community is the place to be. It's a learning ecosystem made especially for technophiles where they can put their toe in the water before jumping into the deep end. Think of it as a Montessori school for engineers.[2]

Early on in her career, Sanghvi adopted a Google mind-set. An engineer by training, she learned to solve problems by working within constraints. But as a businessperson, she learned quickly that she needed to think bigger. South Park Commons is her way of expressing her passion for cultivating the best ideas for the future of technology. In the process, she reinvented her own career.

TWENTY-FIRST-CENTURY LEARNING

The need to learn faster, expand our minds, and rewire our brains for growth is the personal and economic imperative for living in the twenty-first century. To apply a simplistic metaphor, we need to function more like a Swiss Army knife, rather than just a corkscrew or a carving utensil. Organizations are asking their people to work in expanding jobs, pushing them to learn outside of their proficiencies. More and more of these jobs require a combined set of skills, while the half-life of our knowledge and skills is shrinking quickly.

The real challenge today is to stay relevant – to learn how to learn. That's where the Google mind comes in. Curiosity, imagination, and creativity are the core drivers to twenty-first-century learning. Just like Google's search engine, our mind needs to continuously refresh itself. With a Google mind, new insights are created, which expands our possibilities.

The most successful people attribute much of their success to reading. Warren Buffet spends 80% of his day reading. Bill Gates reads 50 books a year. Mark Zuckerberg of Facebook reads one book every two weeks. According to Fast Company, the average CEO reads approximately 60 books per year. They are all expanding their minds every day.[3]

When you encounter something new, your brain tries to fit it into the world you already know. By adding more connections and associations, you expand your understanding. This, in turn, emboldens your creativity. Active curiosity strengthens your brain's wiring.

The opposite is also true. If you do not stretch your brain, certain regions begin to atrophy. This is the principle behind the "use it or lose it" slogan.

Successful entrepreneurs teach us a lot about active learning. They ask a lot of questions to a lot of different people. They shape their future rather than try to predict it. They throw themselves into the sea of unknowns and challenge themselves to swim out. They imagine possibilities before they exist. They learn in public and in relationship with others. They imagine what to do when they don't know how to do it. So how are you learning how to learn? How do you bring rapid growth into your daily life and make it as natural as brushing your teeth?

ACTIVATE YOUR GROWTH MIND-SET

There is a battle raging inside all of us – a battle between our instinctual protective brain and our expanding growth brain. In a rough and tumble world, it is only natural to use our instinctual brain to protect ourselves from danger. But you can't survive and thrive solely with this mind-set. The world is accelerating too fast and we need to be constantly expanding our minds. This requires a growth mind-set, your ticket to twenty-first-century learning and success.

Carol Dweck of Stanford University started this conversation in her groundbreaking book *Mindset*. At Healthy Companies, we expanded this work for application in business. We conducted a project with the Darden School of Business at the University of Virginia to figure out how great leaders succeeded in today's accelerating world. The big differentiator between success and mediocrity was whether people had a growth or a fixed mind-set.[4]

Growth mind-set people see opportunities, think with a broader mind, and prefer action to inaction. They are comfortable with ambiguity, seek out uncertain situations to learn new things, and feel confident they will succeed. Remarkably pragmatic and idealistic at the same time, they view life as a journey of experimentation and continuous learning.

For fixed mind-set people, life is a test. The goal is to pass it without looking foolish or stupid. They feel they are only as good as their most recent performance. They feel compelled to prove themselves over and over. Because they are afraid of exposing their deficiencies, they see criticism and setbacks as indications of their basic flaws. Their primary goal is to avoid making mistakes. They shy away from new experiences and stick to things they know and can do well. Inevitably, this narrows their horizons and shuts down their learning and growth.

The key is to spend as much time as possible in our growth mind-set. But this is not always easy. Our need for certainty, familiarity, and stability keeps us in a fixed place. Old biases and mental models resist change. We also ignore the red flags that tell us it's time to change and learn something new.

Our workplaces also contribute to the problem. Often, we get caught up in the activity trap, stuck in a production mind-set, and don't make time to learn or challenge our thinking. Organizations are designed to reduce risk and promote efficiency. So, we find ourselves challenged by environments that are not conducive to learning. If you want to get unstuck, sometimes you just got to do it yourself.

THE GOOGLE STORY – FROM SEARCH TO ALPHABET

Google is a learning machine. Its purpose, products, and people live the mission, always looking forward to pioneer what's next. The search engine started Google, and the company has evolved into an expanding "alphabet" with subsidiaries as diverse as health care, autonomous vehicles, satellite imaging, venture capital, fiber optic infrastructure, and artificial intelligence. With 74 000 employees, Google is one of the most valuable companies in the world, conducting 1.2 trillion searches each year.

Every year, millions of people tried to get the attention of Laszlo Bock, the senior vice president of Google People Operations from 2006 to 2016. His job was hiring Google's talent during a period of extensive growth. Lore has it that he made Google "Google-y," as one of the primary architects of the company culture. Today, you will find Bock's counterintuitive advice to job seekers plastered online: GPAs are worthless, graduating from college is not a predictor of success, being smart is not enough. What does matter to Bock? "For every job, the No. 1 thing I look for is learning ability. It's the ability to process on the fly. It's the ability to pull together disparate bits of information." It's developing a Google mind.

One of his team members was Chade-Meng Tan, who joined Google in 2000 as an engineer. He was employee #107. For eight years, Tan worked on engineering projects like mobile search. In the spirit of learning, he started teaching Googlers about mindfulness and emotional intelligence during his "20% time," the time Google gives associates to pursue their passions. He could work on anything. It did not need to relate to his core work responsibilities, but it had to benefit the company. Tan eventually joined Bock's People Operations department in 2008 so he could lead his "Search Inside Yourself" workshop full time. This pursuit earned him the Google job title "Jolly Good Fellow."

Tan explains how it all happened: "The secret of my success in Google is to always do the right thing for Google and the world. And then I sit back and wait for them to fire me. If they don't fire me, I've done the right thing. If they do fire me, then I'm in the wrong company. So, either way I win."

After 15 years at Google, Tan retired to run the nonprofit One Billion Acts of Peace. What started for Tan as a side pursuit has now made him a celebrity of sorts. His nonprofit has been nominated for the Nobel Peace Prize eight times; he is a popular TED speaker, an international best-selling author, and a philanthropist. His Google mind lives on.

Sundar Pichai sits at the top of the company. As CEO of Google, he talks a lot these days about thinking big about big problems. Pichai started at Google in 2004 working on Google's search toolbar. He went on to spearhead Google products like Chrome, the Android smartphone, the Chromebook, and Nest – an amazing 13-year track record of launching things people want. "Sundar has a tremendous ability to see what's ahead and mobilize teams around the super important stuff," says Larry Page, Google's founder.

His job is to make sure Google's core businesses (search) and cash cow (advertising) stay strong in the face of growing competition from Amazon, Facebook, and Microsoft. To do that, he has put learning on the top of the company's priority list. Keeping learning about people as important as learning about technology has made Pichai known around Silicon Valley as "proof nice guys can win."[5]

TIPS FOR CONSCIOUS LIVING

Cultivate a beginner's mind.

- Reach back to your younger days, when you were most open and eager to learn. Remind yourself how you felt, the pleasure you experienced of learning something new, having an "Ah-ha" moment, or the excitement of sharing the moment with others. Keep those feelings top of mind. They will help you find motivation (when you're not feeling it) to get unstuck.

Activate the search engine of your mind.

- Tap into your curiosity by taking the time out of your busy days to be curious – stop and wonder for a minute, listen to a podcast, go searching on the web. Realize you are learning, unlearning, and relearning all the time. Make curiosity part of your routine.

Think like an entrepreneur (even if you're not).

- Get out on the diving board and put your ideas into practice. Go where the action is. Start with your own assets and capabilities. Ask yourself, what else can I do with the stuff I already know or have? Use your network to test your ideas. Practice affordable loss – invest only what you are willing to lose.

CHAPTER 15

"And" Is the New "Or"

A high-altitude mountaineer climbs the summit of Mount Everest carrying something that will surprise you. Aside from filling his pack with essentials like bottled oxygen, ice axes, and high-calorie food, he carries a bottle full of little blue pills. That's right, Viagra. Mountaineers experience far fewer cases of frostbite or altitude sickness if they've taken Viagra before entering the "death zone" at the top of Everest.

The history of Viagra is a case study in unexpected discoveries and applications. Researchers were trying to solve the problem of poor oxygen transportation in the body that exacerbated cardiovascular diseases. In the process, they discovered Viagra. Today, Viagra is most famous for treating erectile dysfunction. It also treats patients with lung fibrosis, among other ailments. Without thinking big and exploring multiple uses, Viagra researchers would have produced a failed drug instead of one that is helping millions of people around the world.[1]

A complex world requires a complex mind. Simple "either/or" thinking doesn't cut it anymore. Conscious people excel at "both/and" thinking. They broaden their perspective and create more choices by holding opposing ideas in their heads at the same time.

Many of us think we live in an "either/or" world – colored in black and white, win or lose, us versus them. Framed in simple dichotomies, this "either/or" mind-set narrows our vision, limits possibilities, and reduces choices. It affects how we think, solve problems, and make decisions. It puts us on the defensive when we hear bad news that questions our simple view of the world and keeps us stuck in a narrow mental box.

But we don't live in an "either/or" world. We live in a complex one filled with tensions and opportunities from all directions. You know the constant tug of war between today and tomorrow, long-term goals and monthly targets, managing costs and generating revenues, motivating people and managing performance, and balancing our work and personal lives.

In this complex world, we must think from a broader perspective, examine problems from multiple angles, and develop more creative solutions. Like the story of Viagra, we need to develop a more conscious, bigger approach to solving problems – one that sees the value in "both/and" thinking.

"BOTH/AND" THINKING

Nowadays, what's "right" and what's "wrong" is often obscure. Finding the truth is often complicated. You need a more agile, penetrating mind that understands a more confusing, interconnected life. Decisions are more complex, life is full of contradictions, and there are more risks and opportunities. This is where "both/and" thinking comes to your rescue. It is a powerful tool that enables us to hold all this complexity in our heads at the same time: "'And' is the new 'Or.'"

A paradox exists when two opposing ideas have equal power or truth. Both are real and have merit and yet they contradict each other like good and evil, right and wrong. All the opposites we experience – health and sickness, wealth and poverty, power and submission – are due to the temporary dominance of one principle as the forces toggle back and forth. You can't know happiness if you haven't known sadness.

When confronted by a paradox, "either/or" thinking will get you into trouble. You find meaning and energy from both sides of the continuum, like being reflective and decisive, confident and humble, or realistic and idealistic at the same time. To think big, you must expand and change your reasoning process. Training your mind to use "both/and" thinking allows you to hold multiple ideas in your mind simultaneously. It keeps you from being shackled by polarities and helps you deploy a broader, more inclusive mind.

Our expansive minds have been around a long time, but they get suppressed in our fast-paced, 280-character world. Centuries ago, Buddha made the point with his students using the story of several blind men touching an elephant for the first time. After each blind man felt part of the elephant (tusk, trunk, body, foot, tail), each was asked if he had seen the elephant and to describe what an elephant is. Each blind man firmly believed that his piece of the elephant represented the entire beast. "Either/Or" thinking was touching one part of elephant. "Both/And" thinking brought the whole elephant in focus.

MAKING A CONSCIOUS COMMITMENT

Conscious people are "both/and" thinkers. They set aside biases to explore diverse perspectives. They hold opposing ideas in their heads to develop broadened scenarios. They use the power of paradox as a leadership philosophy in business and life. Jorgen Vig-Knudstorp, CEO of the Lego Group, is a shining example of someone consciously committed to the principle "'And' is the new 'Or.'"

When Knudstorp took over as CEO in 2004, Lego was technically insolvent. Today, as he retires from the company, Lego is very much back in the game and on top of the toy business. Knudstorp attributes this success to his deeply held belief in the power of paradoxical thinking: "There is no single answer to anything anymore – the more ideas evaluated the better." Knudstorp believes growth happens naturally if Lego's leadership stays true to its core paradoxical principles: That the best play involves learning, that creativity requires structure, and that it takes thinking *and* emotions to run a thriving business. Hence, the Lego teams make decisions using the power of broad thinking and deep emotions.

Just as there's no one right way to build a Lego set, Knudstorp chooses to lead and evaluate ideas from many angles to make the best business decisions. One of his favorite mantras, "Take charge and let go," epitomizes this approach. His decision to spend ample company resources on anthropological research enabled his colleagues to learn from customers around the world. Lego creative director Søren Holm likes to say that this dedicated discovery process may be what ultimately saved the company. "We asked an 11-year-old German boy, 'what is your favorite possession?' He pointed to his shoes. When we asked why these were so important, he showed us how they were worn on the side and bottom." The boy explained that the wear and tear on the sneakers showed that he had mastered a difficult skateboarding trick, one that had taken him "hours and hours to perfect."[2]

For the design team, the big takeaway was that Lego blocks (which some felt had become "too easy") should always contain some challenge. To Lego leadership, the story illustrated another useful paradox: Instant gratification isn't always gratifying. We often prefer to be stretched beyond our comfort zones; by doing so, we can demonstrate mastery and stay stimulated at the same time.

For Knudstorp and Lego, "both/and" thinking became their catalyst for innovation, energy for motivation, and driver for long-term growth. Fitting, perhaps, that the Lego name comes from the Danish words for "play well." For Knudstorp, it's both a higher calling and a sound bottom line.

LEADING IN A WORLD OF PARADOX

Imagine you're the sales manager for Viagra in the United States. Your boss just asked you to develop out a sales plan with your team to start to sell the blue pill inside northern China. Wow, what a huge, complex assignment full of paradoxes. Now it's time to put what you learned into practice. Let's first start by using paradoxical thinking inside of you.

- Remain calm *and* challenge yourself with the new assignment.
- Imagine meeting your domestic targets *and* getting to know the Chinese marketplace.
- Use your intellect *and* intuition to figure out how you want to work with your team.
- Feel the anxiety about performing *and* transforming your business.
- Mentally prepare for your first team meeting *and* acknowledge your feelings of excitement and apprehension.

Driving to work this morning, you mentally prepare for your 10:00 a.m. team meeting to launch the Chinese initiative. You've got to figure out how to keep your current clients engaged and happy while we turn our attention to the new markets. Maybe what you really should be worried about is the team. They have so much going on right now. Going into northern China is exciting and scary. The economic and social climate is so different. The tough part is we're not going to be able to hire hundreds of people. As you enter the room, you realize there are a host of paradoxes facing the team.

- How do I balance talking about the opportunity *and* listening to how my team is feeling?
- How can I work with the team using intuitive brainstorming *and* data analytics to understand the market?
- How can I use candor *and* diplomacy to move the team forward?
- How can I be realistic *and* optimistic about the future?
- How do I stay constructive *and* impatient about our deadlines?

Then you turn to the paradoxes inside the company – you've heard the big boss say, "Lead for today *and* tomorrow," "Evolve *and* disrupt your business," "Stay agile *and* disciplined in your leadership."

The paradoxes exist inside you, your team, and the organization. Mastering "'And' is the new 'Or'" will help you survive and thrive in this complex world. Consider these suggestions:

TIPS FOR CONSCIOUS LIVING

Approach challenges as paradoxes.

- Problems are to be solved, paradoxes are to be managed. In a complex world, we need to deal with paradoxes with a "more than one right answer" mind-set.

Identify and explore opposing ideas.

- Stay curious when exploring the opposite viewpoint. Asking, "Tell me more" will help to solicit diverse ideas and cultivate deeper understanding.

List the pros and cons of both viewpoints.

- We tend to focus on the benefits of our perspectives and the limitations of other viewpoints. Consider why you are defensive. Your blinders will narrow your perspective. Another's opinion may broaden your vision.

Look for the "both/and" when making decisions.

- By getting the benefit of opposing viewpoints, you generally will arrive at a better decision. More people will support it, which will help you execute.

CHAPTER 16

Inclusion Is the Road to Innovation

Most of us turn to music or art when we are trying to get inspired. But where do artists go to find their muse when they get stuck? In 1984, finding himself at a low point personally and creatively, Paul Simon went exploring on the other side of the world. He spent two years immersing himself in new sounds and working with new people 7000 miles away from where he'd risen to fame.

After embracing South African music and culture, he produced *Graceland,* arguably his greatest artistic contribution by introducing the sound of African music to the world. It returned Simon to relevance and cemented his place as an iconic artist for generations to come. His genius was in changing his creative process by incorporating diversity, inclusion, and innovation. Adopting this new model of working with others created something truly unique in music. By expanding his palette and working with people from different cultures, he diversified his mind and his art, guaranteeing him superstar status for life.[1]

Simon was an early adopter of cultural inclusion as a path to innovation. Today, we need to do the same thing in our workplaces and our communities. Our borderless, multicultural world requires a deeper appreciation for the diversity around us.

Examine your own life. We brew coffee from Brazil in a pot made in Germany. We take a shower with French soap and wear clothes made in Cambodia. We watch morning news on a TV from Korea, drive to work in a Japanese car, work at a Swedish desk on a Chinese-made computer, and send e-mails from the United States to Australia in less than a second.

As we learn to truly respect our differences in age, ethnicity, and gender, as well as in education, religion, and politics, we broaden our capacity to see the world. We become more mentally and socially agile, gain access to more ideas and choices, and expand our potential and performance.

As Simon experienced, engaging with a diverse group of people jump-started his musical innovations. You might not be a musical superstar nor have the time to take two years off, but you can open your eyes to discover the diversity around you. Tapping into the power of inclusion is good for expanding your mind, and it's good for business. The challenge is that many of us are sabotaged daily by how we think and act.

THE POWER OF UNCONSCIOUS BIAS

To be inclusive, we first must see clearly, with an unbiased mind. Yet bias is as natural to humans as breathing. Many biases are hardwired in our reptilian brain to protect us, like being fearful of a hot burner and not putting your hand on it. Any human thinking or human creation has positive and negative biases. Even algorithms have been shown to have built-in bias because they were designed and coded by humans. The faster the world turns, the more likely we fill our minds with biases to make sense of things. The question we need to ask ourselves is not "Do we have bias?" The real question is "Which biases are mine?" Only then can we take the appropriate action needed to expand our minds.

Unconscious biases are hidden thoughts and feelings we have about other people and situations. These feelings can have no rational basis and yet impact our decisions. For example, if you go into a wine store and hear French music, you're likely to buy French wine. If you hear German music – that's right, German wine. These unconscious biases create a personal subjective social reality. And we have plenty of opportunities to get it wrong, limiting ourselves and hurting others. Social psychologists have identified 175 cognitive biases, organized them into four categories, and explain why we use them.[2]

- We have too much information to process – the Ostrich Effect.
- We reduce the complexity of data – the Simplicity Effect.
- We need to act quickly, but we don't have enough time – the Immediacy Effect.
- We have strong hidden feelings underneath the surface – the Prejudice Effect.

Life moves fast these days. So, we often resort to the cheat sheet of bias to help us make choices quickly. It works much of the time because many biases are good; they simplify our daily life, tap into our past knowledge and experience, and help us make decisions quickly. Unconscious bias also works the other way. Through selective attention, subliminal messaging, and negative biases, our brains only see part of reality. This unfairly stereotypes, prejudices us, and can impose a cultural lens hobbling our worldview.

THE MYSTERY OF MICROAGGRESSIONS

One of the most insidious consequences of bias is "microaggression." Microaggressions are brief, commonplace verbal or behavioral slights, driven by strong biases toward people who are different from you. They can be intentional or unintentional, conscious or unconscious. However, the effects of microaggressions are the same: They serve to alienate people and undermine inclusivity and innovation.

For example, a systems engineering professor might look first at the women in her class to make sure everyone understood the explanation she just gave. She might not be doing it intentionally, but she is reinforcing the idea that she expects her female students not to grasp engineering concepts as quickly as her male students. Microaggressions can be subtle and deeply ingrained as well. Did you read the first sentence of this paragraph and expect it to read "a systems engineering professor might first look at the women in *his* class . . ."?

Negative unconscious bias and microaggressions prevent people from working together effectively. We all need to confront our unconscious biases head-on and operate with a more open and expanded mind. The more inclusive you are about yourself – open to new ideas and accepting your own imperfections – the more inclusive you will be with others, valuing diverse people and eliminating prejudices. Inclusive relationships foster more innovative ideas, allowing you to think bigger.

DIVERSITY LEADS TO INNOVATION

What does this have to do with innovative thinking? If you want to innovate, you need to think like a beginner. Like children, we must learn how to play, to approach the world with open eyes, experiment with fresh ideas, engage with diverse people, and let go of destructive bias. Only then will you begin to discover new ways of doing things.

This is where design thinking comes in. Tim Brown, CEO of IDEO, teaches us how we can learn from designers. "Design thinking is a human-centered approach to innovation that draws from the designer's toolkit to integrate the needs of people, the possibilities of technology, and the requirements of business success."[3] By utilizing empathy and experimentation and challenging the status quo, we can arrive at innovative solutions to new problems. Whether it's improving toothbrushes, feeding the elderly, engaging citizens, or rethinking the restaurant experience, the innovators among us turn abstract ideas into practical applications. Just like Paul Simon did.

Our diverse workplaces and communities are also microcosms of the world. At home, just go to a nearby hospital, a soccer game, or a manufacturing plant and you will see this multicultural world in action. If you are willing to look hard and expand your view of the world, you will find lots of opportunities to innovate.

Yet it's not good enough anymore to look only at our home country for answers. We must also become more globally literate. It starts with being proud of your ancestors, honoring your passport, but avoiding feelings of cultural superiority or inferiority. Then we need to be inquisitive internationalists, looking to other cultures for fresh ideas and practices. As you build relationships with people from other cultures, you become a real student of the global marketplace and the world.

THE ARLINGTON WAY

Where can you find a diverse and innovative community in action? A shining example is Arlington County, Virginia. This urban village pulled off its blinders and buried biases a long time ago. Today, Arlington sits just across the Potomac River from Washington, DC, and has become one of the best places to live and work in the United States. Their vision says it all: "Arlington will be a diverse and inclusive world-class urban community with secure, attractive residential and commercial neighborhoods where people unite to form a caring, learning, participating, sustainable community in which each person is important."[4]

From smart growth and affordable housing to education and sustainability, Arlington embraces a set of values enabling it to walk the talk. Probably their greatest accomplishment is civic engagement. They call it "the Arlington Way." Each person can be an influencer on public policy working toward consensus. Good ideas can come from anyone, and the discussions are governed by a culture of civility and respect. One example is their recent 2050 energy plan. Here government, business, and nonprofit advocacy groups joined forces with citizens to create a sustainable plan for the future.

TIPS FOR CONSCIOUS LIVING

Be aware of your diversity lens.

- Each of us starts with our own cultural biography – influenced by where we are born, our experiences, our background, and our expertise. This lens influences how we see and react in the world.

Confront your unconscious biases and overt prejudices.

- Notice the stories you tell yourself about people and groups and the feelings you have about them. Question your assumptions and explore what is beneath your feelings to identify potential biases.

Be curious about learning from diverse people.

- Ask yourself how each person around you is unique and what is special about their contribution. Be a citizen of your home country, and be open to discovering what other cultures have to offer.

Create a culture of inclusion.

- People enjoy talking about what makes them unique. Practice respect for these differences. It will broaden your perspective and provide more ideas and better solutions.

Plough through obstacles and resistances.

- When you are stuck on differences, keep your higher purpose in mind and create ground rules for communication and decision making.

Tap into the diverse ideas around you.

- Engage in possibility thinking (e.g. "What if . . . "). Be resourceful and creative; find the root cause of a problem and solve it. Test ideas in small ways to experiment and get feedback. Work together to approach opportunities in bolder ways.

Arlington County is one of the most progressive, forward-thinking cities/counties in the world. The county is home to 220,000 people, with more office space available than Denver or San Francisco. Over 100 languages are spoken in the public schools. With a high degree of racial, income, and age diversity, this global village is often described as a big city with a small city feel.

The citizens are 87% satisfied with the county, 35% higher than the national average. And people around the world are noticing. Arlington wins a multitude of awards year after year: Best Place to Live and Work; #1 Digital County in the US; AARP's Best City for Staying Healthy; Best Bike City and Best Green City for Families; Best Walk Friendly Communities; and a variety of cultural, smart growth, and public outreach awards.[5]

Inside Arlington, building a healthy community is not a spectator sport. The leaders and residents achieve all this by being inclusive and innovative – creating a livable community for the twenty-first century. "It is hard work," says county board chair Jay Fisette. "Having created a common vision, and realized that our differences are a key part of our strength, we discovered and unleashed better and more creative ideas and solutions."

PART IV

GET REAL
With Your Accelerators and Hijackers

Today, Elon Musk may be everyone's favorite futurist. In 1999, he struck pay dirt with PayPal when it sold to eBay. It was then that he realized he could change the shape of the future. Musk believes people in the future ought to drive electric cars, fly to Mars, travel between cities in minutes, and live on a sustainable planet. As an inventor, engineer, and investor, he wants to change the world, but he had to Get *Real* first.

Musk's rise to prominence in the worlds of business, technology, aerospace, energy, and transportation illustrates what can be accomplished when you decide to make something happen. To Get Real means to become honest and intentional in your life. It's about learning how to transform yourself and shaping the environment around you. If you can learn how to create the change you desire, you will thrive in a disruptive and accelerating world.[1]

For Musk, it was the experts in the industries he wanted to change that doubted him. In fact, they warned it was he who needed to Get Real. He was told things like: "You can't compete with Detroit by building electric cars." "You can't land a rocket booster on a ship in the middle of the ocean and reuse it." "You can't make better batteries" or "compete with big energy." But Musk persevered by founding companies like SpaceX, Tesla, and SolarCity, and he was determined to disrupt these industries, which were trapped in the doldrums.[2]

Unlike his competitors, Musk took actions that weren't reactive but proactive and deliberate. Rockets are way too expensive, so build a cheaper rocket. Electric car batteries are not strong enough, so build better batteries. Fossil fuels are too polluting, so create smarter energy. Musk listened with a conscious mind and heart and had the courage to transform himself. His businesses followed suit. People said he couldn't do it. But today, few people would be foolish enough to bet against Musk.[3]

Musk is a master of realistic optimism. He sees his vision clearly, yet is honest about what is working and not working. He views the cup as half full versus half empty. He looks beyond the status quo and has the courage to go over, under, and around obstacles to get to his destination. It's this combination of realism and optimism that makes all the difference.[4]

Being realistic is about seeking and speaking the truth – to yourself and others. It's facing problems head-on and being honest about triumphs and failures. Being optimistic is about dreaming about the future. It's about believing that tomorrow will be better than today. When you live and lead with realistic optimism, you can operate in the present and future simultaneously. You have the courage to dream and deliver and trust yourself to create your own destiny.

In "Get Real," you will be challenged to transform yourself. By seeing, thinking, feeling, and acting with a new lens, you will learn to be optimistic and realistic at the same time. You will learn to feed your accelerators and manage your hijackers. You will learn to manage your anxiety along the way. To see a world of possibilities, you will loosen the chains of resistance and become real about the changes you want to make in the future.

Understanding our accelerators and hijackers is the guide for getting real. Accelerators reinforce our good nature. They help us get what we want and teach us to be better people. They move us forward and help to shed light on others. Examples are our courage, drive, hope, optimism, and resilience.

Our hijackers derail us and bring out the worst in us. They keep us stuck, sabotage us, and trigger our most difficult emotions. They make us cast shadows on others. Examples are our controlling nature, our fixed mind-sets, our overly competitive nature, and excessive stress and burnout. Anxiety is our secret weapon. It's our untapped source of energy and the hidden driver of success. We just need to harness the right amount of anxiety to propel us forward instead of tying us in knots.

By getting real, we activate our personal change. Becoming more conscious of ourselves and our surroundings helps us move faster and more thoughtfully into the future.

CHAPTER 17

Transforming Yourself

We must be change agents in our lives, to embrace new challenges, take risks, and reinvent our ourselves. It's up to us to wake up and transform ourselves every day.

There is no better allegory for this than the tale *The Wizard of Oz*. In the story, the main character, Dorothy, travels along the yellow brick road. She becomes a leader, building a diverse team of misfits searching for a wizard who will solve their problems. Yet, there are deep metaphorical currents that run through each character that make this a transformational story we can learn from. The Lion thinks he doesn't have enough courage. The Tin Man thinks he's incapable of forming relationships. The Scarecrow thinks he isn't smart enough to succeed. Finally, Dorothy represents each of us traveling into the unknown with our anxieties.

The characters transform as they travel along the yellow brick road. They become more enlightened, and begin to have more control over their destiny. Their journey is a series of developmental moments of self-discovery. And when they finally meet the Wizard, they realize that they themselves had already solved their problems and made the changes they wanted as they traveled along the road. Like Dorothy, you will experience iterative change along the way as you transform into a more conscious person. But you need to find your own yellow brick road and learn to be conscious of the "gap."

MIND THE GAP

There is a famous announcement in the London Underground: "Mind the gap," loudly and obnoxiously repeating until the train departs. It warns travelers to be conscious of the gap between the station platform and the train they are getting on.

Like riding the train, life entails minding the gap. It is the gap between your current reality (station platform) and your desired future (destination). We are pushed into the gap by our problems and challenges, or whenever we face something we want to fix or change. We are pulled into the gap whenever we seize an opportunity, set goals for ourselves, or dream of a better future. We are navigating the gap when we try to lose weight, learn to be more direct, or work to expand our customer base. This is where your anxiety, creativity, imagination, and energy sit.

In today's fast-paced and competitive world, we must accelerate in the gap – to learn faster and perform better (see Figure 17.1). But the gap is getting more complicated. The distance between our current reality and desired future is widening, and it's harder to move across the gap. When we insist on perfection, resist change, obsess about winning, or hide our real selves, we sabotage ourselves. Fortunately, the more conscious we are, the better we can navigate through the change.

James DePriest was someone who knew how to live and lead in the gap. He was one of the first African American conductors to perform on the world stage, earning him the National Medal of Arts in 2005. What made him unique was his practice of stepping up to the podium with crutches (he had polio), with a mental picture of the ideal performance of his orchestra. In his mind, he could "hear" exactly what the music should sound like, whether he was conducting Beethoven or a concert for children.

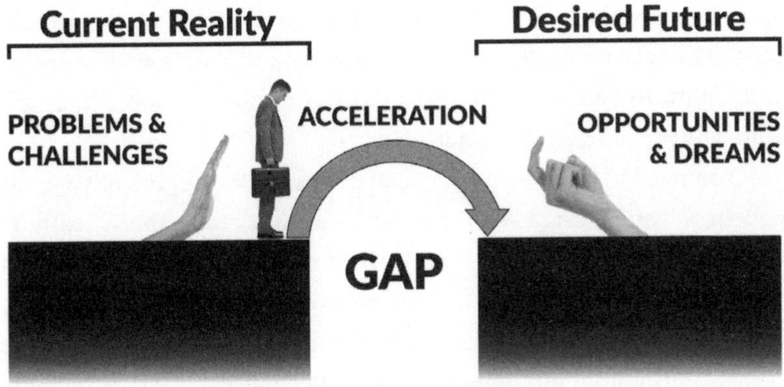

Figure 17.1 Leading and living in the gap.

DePriest constantly compared the ideal performance in his head with the actual performance of his orchestra: "This is going on simultaneously as I listen to the music in the gap. Where is it falling short? Where is it exceeding my expectations?" By comparing the actual with the ideal, DePriest created a reputation for exceptional performances with fans and musicians alike.[1]

We can use the same approach when minding the gap between our current reality and desired future. The challenge is that transformational change is being demanded more these days, with greater frequency. We must surrender our current selves faster and accelerate moving forward.

To move across the gap, we are motivated by either fear or love. When driven by fear, we blame external factors or we blame ourselves. This can result in tripping and falling into the gap, undermining ourselves and lowering our performance. When we are motivated by love and purpose, we effectively navigate across the gap – leveraging our strengths, taking responsibility, and accelerating performance. So how do we actually do this?

YOUR OWN PSYCHOLOGICAL MRI

Now is the time to check yourself – to administer your own diagnostic of your mind. This will give you a snapshot of how you are showing up in the gap. The beauty of the human mind is that it has the mental capacity to rewire itself. By becoming more aware of how this works, you will transform yourself into a more conscious person and accelerate your speed across the gap.

You need to believe you can change the way you think of yourself and how you interact with the world around you. There are four channels for transforming yourself: How we see, think, feel, and act (refer to Figure 17.2). All must work together to create real, sustainable change. This four-step self-exam highlights how your perceptions, thoughts, emotions, and behaviors foster or impede change in your life. Let's examine each one.

Seeing: Acquiring Clear Perceptions

Seeing starts with self-awareness. Can you see yourself and others clearly and honestly? Many of us have difficulty with this channel. We don't have an accurate sense of what we are communicating or how we are perceived. Blind spots, self-absorption, and ancient, immature ego boosts all get in the way. When you lack self-awareness, you hear and see what you want or what you expect – not what is in front of you. Removing these distortions requires looking inside yourself and talking with others. You need an internal and external reality check. Only then can you take off your blinders and accelerate across

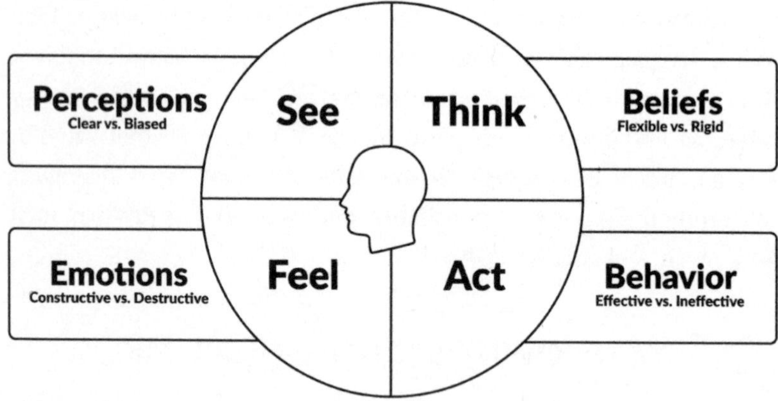

Figure 17.2 Four channels for transformation.

the gap. The key question to ask yourself is: What perceptions about myself and others may be hindering my ability to see clearly?

Thinking: Developing an Open Mind

Thinking starts with clearing your mind. The thoughts you have and the stories you tell yourself will determine whether you engage with an open or closed mind. To move across the gap, you must examine your deep-seated assumptions and beliefs about people and circumstances. If you have a closed mind, you cling to the past and old habits. The result will be fear, bias, and little or no learning. If you open your mind, you explore new ideas and perspectives. You overcome the dangers of overgeneralizing and jumping to conclusions. The result will be hope, understanding, and learning. To be successful in changing yourself, you need to understand your thoughts and how they do or don't serve you. The key question to ask yourself is: What thoughts or assumptions might be dysfunctional or erroneous and getting in my way?

Feelings: Using Emotions Intelligently

Negative and positive emotions have a profound effect on your life. Both are essential for transforming yourself. Negative emotions, like anxiety and loss, are natural feelings during change. But if you don't watch them, they can obscure reality, damage relationships, and threaten your personal health. Remember we all have that alligator, that reptilian brain, ready to jump in and run havoc with our best intentions. Positive emotions act as fuel across the gap. Feelings of hope, faith, forgiveness, and enthusiasm are the gist of creative ideas, a steady moral compass, tolerance, and energy. The key questions to ask yourself are: What persistent feelings might be interfering with my ability to change? What am I doing to moderate my negative feelings and accentuate my positive ones?

Acting: Behaving Constructively

How you act defines you as a person. Your actions make visible what you see, think, and feel. Behaving constructively, both verbally and nonverbally, will determine whether your interactions will have a positive impact. Your most valuable actions are constructive. They contribute something, rather than detract. They build things up and make people feel better instead of tearing them down. They use influence and persuasion instead of domination and deceit. The key questions to ask yourself are: Are my behaviors healthy or unhealthy, constructive or destructive? Are they moving me closer to success?

We differ in whether we are natural seers, thinkers, feelers, or doers. There are many routes to Oz. You can act your way into new ways of thinking, feel your way into new ways of seeing, or think your way into new ways of feeling. Bottom line is, you must develop all four channels to get sustainable behavior change. Start with your strength and build out the other three channels. Leveraging your strengths will help to accelerate the change process.

Perhaps the easiest way to understand our mind in action is to tell you about two leaders, Kevin and Kathie. Both are middle managers going through the feedback phase of their annual 360 development assessment.

Kevin is self-assured and highly vocal about his accomplishments and abilities. He's a big talker and always has an opinion. In any discussion, he often interrupts to interject his own take on events. In his assessment, he gives himself high ratings, thinking of himself as a top performer. He believes this distortion because he generally takes credit for others' accomplishments and over time has come to think they are his. If he makes a mistake or misses a target, he often blames others.

In his dealings with employees, he says he's "spirited and spontaneous." However, colleagues say he's mercurial and unpredictable. He doesn't like to collaborate, fearing that someone will steal his thunder or that he'll lose control of a project. He attributes his lack of team involvement to the shortsightedness of others. When learning about areas he needs to improve on, he becomes angry over some points and glum about others. He argues or challenges the source of the evaluation with the declaration, "That person doesn't know me."

Kevin's learning channels are flawed. His perceptions are blurred, his mind is closed, his emotions are negative, and his actions are unproductive.

Kathie reacts to her assessment differently. Tending to be quiet where Kevin is flashy, Kathie listens more than she talks. She avoids calling attention to herself and often underestimates her abilities. As a result, many of her assessment scores are higher than she expects. She is grateful that others share her belief in long-term planning and the notion that productivity does not happen overnight. She has a broad perspective on success, makes adjustments when events go against her, and is not discouraged by small setbacks.

Throughout the assessment, she is open to what her peers say. Many cite her as a great team player. She enjoys teamwork – bouncing ideas around and working with others to pool their talents and find help for what they can't do. Frequently, she deflects compliments and is generous in her praise of others' good work. The assessment process does not fluster her. Emotionally secure, she's not easily riled or discouraged. Rather, she often laughs at herself. When she hears specific criticisms, she nods in understanding and shows a determination to make changes. At the end, she's appreciative and grateful for the feedback. And although she feels encouraged about her contribution so far, she resolves to redouble her efforts to keep improving.

Kathie's channels are strong and vibrant. Even though her perceptions may be slightly askew or her analysis of situations not always spot-on, she has enough insight to continually sharpen her view of herself.

Many of us are not very good at assessing ourselves. We consciously try to fake or distort the impressions we want to leave on others, or we delude ourselves in believing we are more successful than we are. Here's the fascinating twist. We are much better judges of other people's character and performance than we are of our own. Although some aspects of ourselves can seem invisible, such as our inner thoughts and feelings, research says convincingly that other people are better skilled at assessing us and our performance than we are ourselves. This includes our perceptions, thoughts, feelings, and behavior.

A PERSONAL STORY OF TRANSFORMATION

On October 6, 1998, Judy Shepard's life was changed forever. Her son Matthew was a few weeks shy of his 22nd birthday when he was killed by two thugs in a Wyoming farm field. The reason: Matt was gay. Matthew Shepard's death galvanized a movement to promote equality and freedom in the gay and lesbian communities around the world. It showed hate crimes for what they are.

Matthew's mom, Judy, was by her own admission an "ordinary person," meaning she led a quiet, introverted life with no particular passion or desire to change the world. But her grief, anger, and desire to find justice for her son pushed her into the gap. She transformed into a new Judy, one who fights for social justice, diversity awareness and education, and equality for lesbian, gay, bisexual, and transgender people (LGBT) worldwide. Her horrendous ordeal transformed her so deeply that 20 years later she remains a leader fighting to protect people from hate crimes.[2]

Judy describes her transformation like this: "My friends refer to me as Judy A and Judy B. I'm Judy A with them, which is my old, introverted self who loves to play Mahjong and go to movies with my girlfriends, and I watch a lot of TV, and I read a lot of books. Judy B is out traveling the world and meeting strangers all day, every day, and they still don't understand how this Judy can be that Judy." She explained how she pushed through her introversion to become Judy B: "I was just really pissed. How dare they think they have the right to do that? And how dare people think that it was okay to do that, and not want to address the issue in a more public and aggressive way. It was directed anger. It was my grieving process. It gave me a reason to get up every morning. It allowed me to talk about Matt as much as I wanted. It allowed me to keep him with me and make me feel like I was still part of his life, and his community."

Transforming yourself can be a powerful experience and rewarding for yourself, the people around you, and society. Judy saw reality with clear eyes. She opened her mind to possibilities. And she consciously directed her anger in constructive ways. Judy's passion and willingness to become a public figure resulted in new federal hate crime laws being enacted, further protecting our society from bigotry. She continues to fight injustice from Wyoming while traveling the world.[3]

CHAPTER 18

The Three Faces of Anxiety

Anxiety is a fact of life. How you use it makes all the difference. If you let it overwhelm you, it will turn to panic. If you deny or run from it, you will become complacent. Using anxiety in a positive way will turn it into a powerful force in your life.

Remember when you were a kid. One of your friends zapped you with a rubber band. Ouch! You learned quickly that rubber bands can be deadly, releasing their potential energy on you with a vengeance. Most of us still can't resist shooting a rubber band. We know that if we stretch it too far, the band will snap and slap us. When we don't stretch the band enough, it will go limp and fall at our feet. To make the rubber band soar across the room, we need to put just enough tension into it so it has sufficient energy to go where we want it to strike.

The rubber band metaphor captures the essence of how to live with our anxiety, a clear side effect of our fast, disruptive world and the stress in our daily lives. Uncertainty is reality and anxiety is our natural partner. Yet it is imperative that we get real about our anxiety. Successful people understand that the bigger threat to peace of mind is not anxiety itself, but rather the way we perceive it.

Most of us view anxiety through a purely negative lens. We see anxiety as something to fear and avoid. This thinking is self-defeating and can even make us more anxious. So why is it so difficult to deal with anxiety? It starts with faulty thinking and can go something like this: Uncertainty makes me anxious. I feel vulnerable. Anxiety leads me to worry or run away. Now I'm no longer in control of my life and that feels even worse.

Our faulty thinking comes from centuries of viewing change as dangerous, even life-threatening. It comes from medical models that frame anxiety as solely a mental health problem. And it comes from years of outmoded leadership practices that ignore the human side of business. These notions about change and anxiety are not helpful today.

Instead, what we need to do is see anxiety as a wake-up call, a message inside our body telling us to pay attention. Clearly, excessive anxiety needs to be treated by a professional. Yet, for many of us, anxiety is a source of stored energy that can be used to our advantage. Getting real about anxiety leads you to uncover the hidden driver of life and business success.

To accept anxiety as a natural part of the human experience is to get real about what living consciously actually means. Like a rubber band, too much anxiety will cause us to snap. Too little anxiety and we stay stuck. Living and leading with just enough anxiety is where we want to be.[1]

There are three faces to anxiety: Too little, too much, and just enough. Too little anxiety is the face of complacency. Too much anxiety is the face of chaos. Just enough anxiety is the face of success. Let's take a look at each one.

TOO LITTLE ANXIETY: THE FACE OF COMPLACENCY

Having too little anxiety is like living with your head in the sand. You naturally avoid change and value the status quo. Not surprisingly, people like this tend to live in a bubble. They may have been spared from difficulty for most of their lives. Or they may have learned at an early age to protect themselves from the complexity and uncertainty that surrounds them. Needless to say, this doesn't work in today's volatile world. It's like wearing a self-imposed blindfold. It keeps you from having to face difficult problems and limits your ability to learn. In our travels, we have observed four different ways people express too little anxiety at work and in life.

Idealistic people *live in a fantasy world.* Driven by their need to have things work out favorably, they tend to ignore reality and gloss over bad news. "Everything will work out just fine" is their go-to platitude. Idealistic people need to learn how to look reality straight in the eye, while not losing their ability to be positive and optimistic.

Cautious people *are frightened by the world.* Driven by their fear of change and uncertainty, they overcompensate by trying to avoid everything. They need to feel totally certain before they take action, leading to indecision and perpetual procrastination. Lacking the sense of urgency needed to stay competitive, they are afraid of taking risks. Their go-to platitude is "I need all the facts before I can decide." Caution can be a virtue, but these folks need to focus less on stability and learn to take more risks.

Detached people *isolate themselves from the world.* Driven by the need to protect themselves, they operate best on their own or with minimal interaction. Their go-to platitude is "I'll take care of it. No need for you to be involved." Many withdraw entirely from tense situations and difficult relationships. Their cool demeanor can be mistaken for arrogance. Being intelligent is meaningless if you are socially handicapped. Detached people need to learn to make deep emotional connections along with their logical and objective selves.

Overpleasing people *live in other peoples' worlds.* They are driven by the need to make everyone happy. They are uncomfortable with conflict and using their own power to influence others. This makes them great people-pleasers. Over time, they lose their identities and undermine their own authority. Their go-to platitude is "Let me check with others and get back to you." Overpleasing people need to get along with others yet need to learn how to be assertive and step up for themselves and their people.

You might want to ask yourself whether you are a too-little-anxiety person?

- Do you feel uncomfortable with growth and change?
- Do you try to give everyone what they want?
- Do you believe everything will turn out okay or resolve itself?
- Do you find it hard to get in touch with your emotions?
- Do you naturally shy away from conflict?

The economics of too little anxiety can also be devastating. Difficult issues get ignored. Projects start and stop unpredictably. People waste time in unnecessary activities. Ask yourself: Do you work for a too-little-anxiety leader? Does your organization lack a sense of urgency? Does talent go untapped or underutilized? Is mediocre performance tolerated? Do you miss out on opportunities? If so, now might be the time to stir things up.

TOO MUCH ANXIETY: THE FACE OF CHAOS

Most of us are too familiar with too much anxiety. Today's frenetic world makes it difficult to avoid. But some people are vulnerable to making too much anxiety a habit. The problem is that many of these people are overly attached to success. Their need to be exact, right, powerful, or in control of their world drives their behavior and creates unhealthy energy around them. Behind this attachment is fear – the fear of inadequacy, failure, insignificance, or being taking advantage of.

Emotionally, too-much-anxiety people are out of touch with themselves in the moment. Inside they are frequently held hostage by their emotions – anxiety, anger, sadness, and fear. Yet they wear their feelings on their sleeves. Their emotional transparency is the problem: They bring their inner chaotic energy to everyone around them. Here are four types we have observed in our work:

Egotistical people *want the world to revolve around them.* They are driven by two needs: To be admired and to protect themselves from their feelings of inadequacy. Ironically, they are often good at what they do, but their inflated view of their talents and importance leads them astray. Weaknesses, their own and others', are not tolerated. Or, they surround themselves with "yes" people to reinforce their egos. Their go-to platitude is "My way or the highway." Egoists need to continue to act with pride and confidence yet must learn to listen to and respect others.

Perfectionistic people *try to orchestrate the way the world works.* They are accomplished micromanagers. Underneath the surface, they are driven by the fear of failure or are insecure about not being good enough. Their attention to detail is a great asset that makes them accomplished micromanagers. From their perspective, there's always one way to do things. Anything that deviates from their personal standard produces a high level of anxiety in them and frustration in those around them. Their go-to platitude is "Let me take one more pass at this." The drive for excellence is a positive impulse, yet they need to accept imperfections in themselves and others.

Volatile people *believe the world is against them.* Driven by the desire to win at any costs, second place is unacceptable. They wield their power like an emotional saber, cutting down whatever and whoever gets in their way. They make decisions solely to further their own interest, letting the consequences fall where they may. Their go-to platitude is "Are you with me or against me?" Volatile people need to remain competitive yet need to recognize that "no man is an island."

Suspicious people *are mistrustful of the world around them.* Their own suspicious nature leads them to believe that people are inherently dishonest. Given the chance, they think people will take advantage of them. Suspicious leaders are hijacked by their mistrust. They project it outward and it comes back full circle. They create a culture where distrust, accusation, and deception are the norm. Their go-to platitude is "Are you telling me the truth?" Knowing how to question is important, but they must learn to trust and be open to others.

So, ask yourself, are you a too-much-anxiety person?

- Do you expect to be respected and admired?
- Do you feel tense and frustrated much of the time?
- Do you question other people's motives?
- Do you get overly impatient with others?
- Do you wear your emotions on your sleeve?

Too-much-anxiety leaders create too-much-anxiety teams and organizations. It shows up all over the place. Creative, take-charge people feel suffocated. Resentment and frustration fills the air. Information is withheld and mistrust is the norm. Ask yourself, do you work for a too-much-anxiety leader? Is your organization in a crisis all the time? Are people punished for mistakes and failures? Is poor morale a daily reality? If so, you might want to take your boss to the gym to work off some tension and carefully share your thoughts about how he is undermining his own success.

JUST ENOUGH ANXIETY: THE FACE OF SUCCESS

Just enough anxiety is the right level of tension that drives you forward without causing you to resist, give up, or try to control what happens. It unleashes your productive energy and makes you want to do better. Just enough anxiety creates the optimal condition for learning so you can stretch beyond your current reality into your desired future. It allows you to close the gaps in your life – gaps between who you are and who you wish to be, and between where your organization is and where you want it to be.

What do you see when you look in the mirror? Do you see the face of complacency? The face of fear? Or do you see the face of acceleration? You've probably seen all three at different times in your life.

We all lean toward too little or too much anxiety under stress. Some of us are drawn repeatedly into too much anxiety. Others of us gravitate toward too little. Nobody remains in the middle all the time. Your goal is to maintain your balance. Getting diverted from the middle for too long has dramatic consequences for you. Too little anxiety produces ineffective energy. Too much anxiety generates chaotic energy. Only just enough anxiety accelerates your path toward sustainable success.

Why is this so important? Because anxiety is contagious. Our brains are hardwired to pick up cues from our environment, including other people. We unconsciously monitor tone of voice, facial expressions, body language, eye contact, attentiveness, and other nonverbal cues. We interpret people's behavior. We sense their intentions. We feel their feelings. And they feel ours.

We are simply hardwired to be connected to each other. We mirror what we see in others. Our cells help us connect with each other. Your leadership style can affect people's health. Studies show that people's blood pressure goes up dramatically when they deal with a manager who is disrespectful, unfair, or insensitive. It remains normal when they work with a leader who is respectful, fair, and sensitive.

MAKING ANXIETY WORK

Mark Madgett knows the power of just enough anxiety. A veteran of New York Life Insurance Company, which was founded in 1845, Madgett started his career as a life insurance agent 31 years ago. Few know more about anxiety than salespeople, especially when you're selling life insurance to families discussing life-and-death issues.

Today, Madgett runs this Fortune 100 company's agency with a field force of 12 000 career agents. It's not easy to evolve and disrupt a 172-year-old company, and Madgett is the man to pull it off. His first assignment is to guide the agency to embrace a digital ecosystem, moving from products to solutions, transactions to relationships, and analog to digital. A true transformation in the gap.

"Change is one of those words that causes real emotional reactions," says Mark as he speaks to his colleagues at a 2017 Agency Town Hall meeting. "It can be exciting and full of promise or it can be scary and full of fear."

"It's critically important that we get the right mindset about change. We fall into two basic camps. You can believe that *change is happening to me* and ask yourself who or what can I blame. Or you can believe that *change is happening for me*, where you can grow and lean into the future."

"If you want to see opportunity, we must make a conscious effort and an emotional commitment to owning the journey from the inside out. We must first steward ourselves before we can change the organization."

Madgett is comfortable talking about the company's purpose, bold goals, business strategy, and great execution. But his real energy comes alive when he shares his own thoughts on what's going on inside us. "We are always in negotiations with our positive and negative self. Most human beings have greater than 90% self-defeating thoughts, and these show their ugly head when change happens. To move ourselves into positive self-talk we must consciously interrupt ourselves."[2]

Here you find a leader discussing what really happens during change and transition. It's where drive, learning, strategy, and awareness come together. It's the work we do in the gap. This is at the heart of living and leading with just enough anxiety.

CHAPTER 19

Feed Your Accelerators

In India, there is a 125-year-old lunch delivery service called the dabbawala network. Thousands deliver home-cooked, hot food in lunch boxes to office workers in Mumbai every day. It is claimed that the "lunch box men" make less than one mistake in every six million deliveries. What drives these delivery men to be such a phenomenon in supply chain management?

Their secret: The dabbawala guys drive with their personal accelerators – the passion for what they do, the meaning they find in their work, and their desire to live up to their history and reputation. These delivery men choose to see, think, feel, and act every day in a manner that allows them to feel deep pride in their work. For them, pride take precedence over a paycheck.[1]

Accelerators drive us forward. They activate positive energy and support us to move across the gap. The more aware we are of our accelerators, the more we can use them to activate change. Our hijackers do the opposite. They undermine and sabotage us and derail us in negative ways. Accelerators put us in the driver's seat. Hijackers slow us down and apply the brakes.

What is needed to create real change in our lives and inside organizations is to raise awareness about what accelerates us forward. Examples could include our hope and optimism, confidence and generosity, or focus and practice. Our hijackers are things like perfectionism, pleasing others, and stress and burnout. We will talk about your hijackers in Chapter 20.

To get a clearer picture of how our accelerators work, let us introduce you to Major General Tammy Smith.

What does Major General Smith do in the US Army? "I'm responsible for the strategic vision, resources, and leadership that drives large numbers of people to achieve our goals." In other words, making things happen is Smith's job. So how did this career soldier, a woman who happens to be a lesbian, navigate through the trials and tribulations of a male-dominated military hierarchy? By using her accelerators to drive herself forward – by being true to her principles, staying confident, and displaying strong leadership presence.

As a young officer, people saw Smith's soft-spoken, collected demeanor as not how you lead soldiers. They suggested she be more aggressive and confrontational. Some people even went as far as implying that she wasn't leadership material. But Smith was unfazed: "My leadership style is based on my character, my values, my self-awareness, how I interact with people. It is a collaborative leadership style. But at the entry level in the Army, what you picture is the drill sergeant. The high and tight haircut, the loud hollering, directing squads into combat under fire. I did not fit that at all."

Smith didn't cave under the pressure. She didn't get hijacked by stereotypes. She stayed true to who she was as a leader. Relying on her principles of kindness and fairness made it possible for her to collaborate more effectively with her soldiers. She left no room for argument with the results she achieved. This got her noticed by her superiors and accelerated her up the chain of command.

Leadership presence can be described as the ability to be calm under pressure – to be bold yet wise, fast yet careful, decisive yet prudent. Says the general, "I make sure that my leader presence is always well rehearsed."

In South Korea today, Tammy leads in a world where stability is an illusion. She reflects, "There is a great deal of uncertainty out there. Sometimes it can feel chaotic. A person must get her stability internally. My personal approach is to bring a level of sameness to the organization by being consistent with my calming presence."

Smith entered the US Army at a time when women were just beginning to be integrated into the organization. By using her quiet confidence, deep-rooted principles, and unwavering leadership presence, she didn't lose faith in herself. "No. I doubled down. I love serving, being in uniform, and being a military leader."[2]

ACCELERATORS IN ACTION

Let's look at five common accelerators in more detail: Courage, drive, practice, resilience, and vulnerability.

Courage

In *The Wizard of Oz,* the Cowardly Lion desperately wanted courage. Chased by his personal fears, he continuously doubted himself with his tail between his legs at every uncertainty. What the Cowardly Lion shows us is that courage is not the absence of fear. Rather, courage is moving forward in spite of your fear. Being courageous means practicing grit and persistence to face difficult situations with grace and dignity.

We all want courage and we all celebrate courageous acts. Courage can come in many forms: You may follow your heart or your intuition, you may face fear head-on and choose to act, you may stand up for what is right, or you may persevere in the face of adversity. When faced with constant change, having courage may be your best prescription. Courage is not something you are born with. You need to practice being courageous so that it will be there for you when the going gets tough.

Questions to reflect on:

- How would you show up and what would you be doing if you were more courageous?

- Who do you admire who demonstrated great courage? What could you emulate about them?
- How could practicing courage help you to thrive in uncertain times?

Drive

Drive is having and showing the motivation and commitment to achieve your goals in life. Additionally, drive, desire, and practice are wonderful bedfellows. When they are connected to making a choice, something powerful happens. We proactively learn new things, develop new habits, and change our behavior.

Drive is a go-to accelerator for leaders. Let's face it. We all want to be successful and we want to work for or be around successful people. Winning, getting ahead, achieving goals, making a difference – these make us feel better about ourselves. When we set specific and difficult goals, we get better performance because we use that extra dose of determination. Success comes from a combination of factors – from character and talent to ambition and practice. Drive is the common fuel that moves us forward.

Questions to reflect on:

- What drives you forward? What engages your heart and inspires you to action?
- How might having more drive help you to be more effective in an accelerating and disruptive world?
- Do you schedule your most difficult tasks when you have high energy and limited time?

Practice

Change requires focus, attention, repetition, *and* practice. We're talking about deliberate practice! All great performers – in sports, music, entertainment, and yes, leadership – practice intensely. Experts are made, not born.

You start with a challenge or opportunity and lay out a proposed path toward your desired future. Practicing the same behaviors enough times will enable your mind to become a habit-forming machine. Research says that to be successful at something, you need to work long and hard, pause and reflect with proper mindfulness, and regularly engage in deliberate practice.[3]

The key is to focus. Our mind has a tendency to get distracted when bombarded with lots of external stimulation. So when we practice, it's important to focus our mind. Deliberate practice is about challenging yourself slightly above your competency level, repeating yourself, and getting real time feedback.

Questions to reflect on:

- When did you last deliberately set about improving what you do? How did you create new habits?
- What is it that distracts you when engaging in deliberate practice?
- How could you incorporate real-time feedback and sufficient challenge into your practice habits?

Resilience

Resilience is being able to recover quickly from setbacks and adversities. How resilient are you? Most likely, you underestimate your strength to rebound quickly. You are much more resilient than you think. Resilience is like a muscle that must be exercised. The more you use it, the stronger it becomes.

Whether you are coping with adversity, bouncing back from setbacks, or leading through uncertainty, these experiences can make you stronger. When you rise to a challenge, you reveal your hidden ability, strengthen your capacity to suffer through setbacks, and build character. Adversity's impact on your consciousness makes you more sensitive to others and gives you deeper and greater perspective.

Questions to reflect on:

- When was the last time I fell down and got up? What did I say to myself?
- How do I consciously maintain my resilience in the moment? Where does my mind wander? How does fear get in my way?
- In a disruptive environment, what can help me get up more quickly? How do I increase my capacity to self-correct?

Vulnerability

In the eyes of others, you are more likeable, more trustworthy, and more authentic when you allow yourself to be vulnerable. Really. It sounds very counterintuitive, but being willing to accept and show your uncertainty or weaknesses is your strength. It's not wearing your heart on your sleeve. Rather, it is understanding that authenticity trumps hubris. Trying to be your most honest and open self will accelerate you forward.

You might be surprised that vulnerability is an accelerator. Most people feel it is a sign of weakness, a flaw in your character, and a recognition of failure. But that is old thinking. In a world of uncertainty, we are all vulnerable. Many people, especially men, run away from or work hard to hide their vulnerability by never showing their emotions, weaknesses, or mistakes. But people are hungry to be with real people, who expose themselves emotionally and show up as real human beings.

Questions to reflect on:

- In what way will facing vulnerability bring you release, strength, truth, and peace of mind?
- What weaknesses can you accept and share with others? How would doing this make you feel?
- What is your reaction to people who express vulnerability? Do you judge them, or does it feel safer being around them?

PUTTING YOUR ACCELERATORS TO WORK

How can you embrace and use these accelerators at work and in your daily life? Let's check in with Barry, a participant in one of our Conscious Leadership workshops. Barry is using vulnerability as an accelerator to transition into a new leadership job.

"Not meaning to toot my own horn, but I'm going from a place where I walked on water to a place where, from the get go, I'll be in over my head. My company is growing fast and has asked me to make a big change. Honestly, it's a scary time for me. For much of my career, I've been a programming star leading high-profile projects to successful completion. My people skills are good. I get along well with others and people come to me for help all the time, on technical issues. Now, in this new senior leadership role, I must quickly transition from a 'doer' (which I enjoy doing) to 'leading' others to do the work and focusing more on strategic issues. I have mixed feelings of excitement and trepidation.

"My staff knows that this is all new for me. I don't want to be somebody that I'm not. They will see right through me. The best way to move forward is to be honest about my vulnerability. First, I want my team to know it's okay to tell me if I'm not listening or I'm being too controlling. I need to learn to be hands-off on the technical stuff and let my staff take the lead. I'm no longer the de facto tech guy. Now my job is to create the next tech stars and have them flourish and grow under my leadership. My goal is for our team to build a camaraderie based on mutual respect and understanding that helps us achieve success for the company. I can do this by using vulnerability as an accelerator and not let my anxiety force me to overcompensate."

What's going on with Barry?

- He's *seeing* himself clearly. Barry is honest about being a neophyte executive. He understands correctly that people know him well and they will question any ounce of hubris or deception. They also like him and want him to succeed. Why not be honest and a little vulnerable?
- He's *thinking* with an open mind-set. Having an open mind in the new job is critical to his success. Barry will need to question some of his assumptions about his role and responsibility, what he knows and doesn't know, and be honest about his steep learning curve.

- He's *feeling* positive about the opportunity. Anxiety naturally shows up when you walk into an unknown job. Why not acknowledge it to yourself and talk about it with others? Most people will give you points for being honest.
- He's *acting* constructively in the new job. Try to experiment with new behaviors. You may not get them right at the start, but practice will give you confidence and people will see you working toward a desired outcome.

CHAPTER 20

Befriend Your Hijackers

In sports, there are rare athletes who stand above, giants who tower over even the greatest who came before and after them. Michael Phelps at age 24 seemed to be in the company of transcendent figures like Babe Ruth, Pelé, and Joe Montana. But what happened to Phelps is an old story: An incredibly talented person dedicates his life to the pursuit of excellence and achieves the pinnacle of professional success, only to fall prey to life's hijackers once he reached the top.

Discovered at age 11 by Bob Bowman, his long-term coach, Phelps first got his feet wet at the Sydney Olympics in 2000. At age 15, he was the youngest male to make the US Olympic swimming team in 68 years. Four years later, in the 2004 Athens Olympics, he won his first gold medal.[1] Phelps didn't just win one gold medal; he won six golds and two bronze medals, thoroughly establishing himself as a phenomenon. He returned in 2008 to dominate the Beijing Olympics. He didn't disappoint, taking home eight gold medals and breaking records, including Mark Spitz's seven golds in a single Olympic Games. Beijing left Phelps feeling as if he was "in a dream world." But unbeknownst to millions of spellbound fans around the world, there was trouble brewing in the water.[2]

In 2009, a photograph surfaced of Michael Phelps using marijuana. The image was the first step in a very public downward spiral for the Olympian. The years that followed Phelps's astonishing eight-gold-medal performance at the Beijing Olympics were quickly overshadowed by scandal. Multiple DUIs, drugs, alcohol, strained and broken relationships – these were the things that began to define the new Michael Phelps.[3]

It is not without some irony that in 2014, Phelps was arrested by police for going too fast in an underwater tunnel. He was driving 84 mph through Baltimore's Fort McHenry Tunnel, under the influence of alcohol. On October 6, 2014, USA Swimming banned Phelps from competing for six months. In addition, Phelps would not represent the USA at the 2015 World Aquatics Championships. When later interviewed by *Sports Illustrated,* Phelps said, "I knew I was going to get suspended. I didn't know they were going to take World's away. I didn't even know that was an option."[4]

In her *New York Times* article "Seeking Answers, Michael Phelps Finds Himself," writer Karen Crouse says, "By the end of 2014, it appeared plain to everyone that the trail Phelps blazed had veered into a dead end." This landed him at The Meadows, an Arizona inpatient treatment facility. "I was so afraid coming in," Phelps said. "I wasn't ready to be vulnerable. And then, after a couple of days, I said: 'My wall is down. Let's get into this and see what is going on.'" In rehab, Michael was able to be honest with himself to discover who he really was. His stay at The Meadows brought to the surface many of the issues that hijacked him.[5] Phelps, like many talented people, was plagued by personal hijackers. What led to his fall from grace?

"I didn't see me as me," Phelps said in his *NYT* interview with Crouse. "I saw me as everybody else did – as an all-American kid. Let's be honest. There's not a single human being in the world that's like that."[6] Needing to be special can be an insidious hijacker, which likely undermined Phelps's ability to see himself as a whole person. In therapy, he decided that he no longer wanted to be how others defined him. He wanted to be Michael Phelps the person, not Michael Phelps the Olympian. He pledged to himself that the world would see him for who he was, glories, faults, and all.

Another hijacker Phelps discovered in rehab was his fixation on success. This a catch-22. If Phelps hadn't been so fixated on becoming the world's greatest swimmer, he almost certainly wouldn't have achieved what he did. However, being driven by an overwhelming need for achievement at all costs took a heavy toll on him. Phelps described his decline as inevitable and said: "It's like we dreamed the biggest dream we could possibly dream and we got there. What do we do now?"[7] These feelings of being lost led him to look for an escape, which he found in drugs and alcohol.

Perfectionism in sports doesn't translate to life. It took until Phelps's crisis for him to realize that being the perfect swimmer didn't make him a whole human being. Perfectionism is not possible – that's why it's a hijacker. There is a difference between striving for excellence and pursuing perfection. One nurtures ambition. The other borders on obsession. It's a slippery slope we face when trying to achieve something. The more conscious we are, the more we can make the distinction.

At the 2016 Rio Games, Phelps rose to the top of the podium once again as an Olympic champion, winning five gold medals and one silver – and bringing him up to 31 gold medals in total. His mother, wife, and son Boomer were right by his side as he celebrated the best in history while enjoying the fruits of being just an everyday guy.[8]

Phelps is a poster child for life's accelerators. Drive, desire, practice, focus, resilience, and confidence – these are all written into his DNA. However, like all of us, he is human and equally susceptible to life's hijackers. Phelps's rehabilitation helped him wake up and see that even the best in the world need to work hard to be more conscious.

THE JOB OF HIJACKERS

In a disruptive and accelerating world, we are all vulnerable to being hijacked. Just about anything can kick us off center – disruptors and distractions, wanting to escape and ignoring reality, getting lost in our emotions and being blinded by our thoughts. Wherever we turn, our hijackers are lurking just under the surface.

Hijackers function a lot like Homer's sirens. We are easily lured by them and end up being tossed on the rocks. When we stop to look around, we notice our hijackers are controlling us versus us controlling them. We undermine our best selves and weaken our credibility and our leadership.

Like a vicious cycle, our hijackers activate our brains. Our reptilian brain responds with a fight-or-flight response when it perceives a threat. Stress chemicals like cortisol, adrenaline, and norepinephrine are released. This increases anxiety, sleeplessness, pain, and depression, ultimately reinforcing the use of more hijackers. Once we become aware of what happens, we can choose a different response.

Hijackers come in many forms – worrying too much, wallowing in disappointments, or getting angry when things don't go our way. In some instances, it's certain kinds of people that hijack us – arrogant people, controlling people, selfish people. In some situations, we bring up old memories from the past and we get hijacked the same way we did before. Other times, it's simply how we think that hijacks us – our obsession with winning, our tendency to be controlling, or our perfectionistic style. The key is to be conscious when you get hijacked, and to recognize the impact it has on your health and performance.

HIJACKERS IN ACTION

Let's look at five common hijackers: Being self-critical, having a cynical attitude, being too controlling, staying aloof, and harboring an overly competitive mind-set.

Self-Criticism

Self-deprecation is a very effective tool of comedy but a tragedy for those of us prone to it. Yet many of us are vulnerable to blaming ourselves for the disruptions around us. Are you hard on yourself? Do you criticize yourself and everything you do? Do you always look for ways you were responsible for a problem? These are common attributes of self-critical people. People who are hijacked by self-criticality have trouble expressing their full power in the world and push people away by their poor self-esteem.

We all need to check ourselves and use our inner critic but not let it run amok. Self-criticism can be dominated by perfectionism, abusive relationships, and impossible scenarios. Whenever you find yourself doubting your capability, be sure your inner critic isn't on steroids.

Questions to reflect on:

- Notice when you are self-critical. What triggers these thoughts? What other thoughts could you replace them with?
- Where do you feel the impact in your body? Do you feel yourself shrinking?
- Find the real reason for your self-criticism. What is it that you are afraid will happen? How realistic is that?
- When do you feel good about yourself and consider you have done a great job?

Cynicism

In a world of mistrust and "alternative facts," cynicism becomes a popular commodity. Doubting others and questioning people's motives becomes the norm. It's another frequently used comedic trope. But everyday cynicism is no laughing matter. It grinds you down and can sap your energy and joy. It is the primary indicator of burnout at work.

Many of us try to hide our feelings or not let them interfere with our leadership and life. But hiding gets tougher every day. We might be angry at our boss or the company, frustrated with our staff, anxious about our family, or just cynical or burned out. If your level of engagement is not in top form, you can rest assured that the people around you will notice and feel it. A recent poll by the Gallup Organization reported that 70% of workers feel emotionally disconnected from their employers and are less productive than they could be.[9]

So, if your personal engagement with others is off and you don't know why, you may be getting hijacked by being too cynical.

Questions to reflect on:

- When does sarcasm, doubt, or mistrust turn to cynicism in your life? What happens to you both mentally and physically? What is the impact on others?
- What lies behind your cynicism? Is it your personality or a long history of disengagement?
- Might you be facing reduced resilience and/or burnout? What are you doing to nurture yourself?

Being Too Controlling

As the world gets more uncertain, the less control we have over it. Yet, in a strange way, the less control we have, the more we want to grasp for it. Let's face it: Feeling an intense need to influence and shape your environment is common to all of us. However, grasping doesn't serve us well in modern times. The more we grasp, the less control we actually have. Beware that a heavy-handed desire to control can come at the expense of yourself and others. Whether by forcing your perspective upon others or micromanaging them, being too controlling is a surefire hijacker of relationships. And you may lose yourself in the process.

A high need for control looks like this: Judging, criticizing, or correcting people when they are wrong; always trying to win an argument; refusing to admit a mistake or flying into rages. You may be a part of contributing to a toxic environment where productivity is reduced and job satisfaction suffers.

Questions to reflect on:

- What is the difference for you between influencing and controlling? Where is the line? How do you distinguish between these?
- Do you trust or mistrust your team or friends? When you do either, how do you feel?
- If you could dial this hijacker down, what would your actions look like?

Aloofness

If this hijacker were an animal, it would certainly be a cat. You know the stereotype – the dog wants to be your best friend and a cat is cautious, keeping his distance to protect himself.

It's only natural to want to protect yourself from the frantic, crazy world we live in. But people who are aloof create a feeling that they don't care about others, causing both separation and alienation. They generate feelings of contempt, and this makes others feel inadequate.

People are hungry for connection. When you are aloof, you put distance between yourself and others. You could be perceived as reserved and detached, unapproachable in social situations, or emotionally cold. Generally, this hijacker is driven by the fear of intimacy and human connection. Aloof people are distant and detached without even knowing it.

Questions to reflect on:

- How might this hijacker constrain your career if you don't address it in our connected world?
- Who do you feel closest to at work? How did you make that happen? What can you take from this experience and apply to others?
- When did you last socialize with colleagues? How might you reach out and spend time with them? What might happen if you did?

Hypercompetitiveness

It's so easy to be lured by the spirit of competition. It's everywhere these days, whether it's the next pay raise, a jump in stock price, competing against coworkers, or simply being the most generous person at church. Healthy competition fuels our energy and accelerates performance. But when the need to win takes precedence over everything else, we can lose ourselves, our friends, and our opportunities.

Some of us get seduced by a win/lose mentality and miss out on the potential for partnerships and alliances. Jealousy, envy, and lack of generosity take hold. Others keep plenty of balls in the air to protect themselves from feelings of failure and inadequacy. Still others get lost on the island of self-interest and develop a reputation for being "out for themselves." There is little evidence that being hypercompetitive makes for better success.

Questions to reflect on:

- What effect does this hijacker have on your life and leadership?
- When it intrudes, how does it take over? How might you stop that?
- How can you tune up or tone down your competitive spirit? What strengths and vulnerabilities do you bring to bear?
- What will you do differently? And what will the payback of that be?

BEFRIEND YOUR HIJACKERS

How can you befriend and manage your hijackers at work and in your life? Let's check in with Brooke, a participant in one of our Conscious Leadership workshops. As a leader, Brooke is dealing with a history of employee morale problems and is getting tired of it. She's struggling with a fixed mind-set, a situation where her beliefs, abilities, and circumstances cannot be changed – at least, so she thinks.

"What is wrong with these people?! I'm doing a great job considering who I have to work with. The projects are more complicated and people are not stepping up. They go home early and are complaining about me and the work. They don't understand how leadership works or the pressures I'm under. I must get the job done. I'm so tired of hearing that I don't listen to my people. Now I'm going to have to put up with the 'be a better leader' lecture from my boss again. This is so frustrating.

"My coach tells me I need to look at this differently. He says, I should turn the problem upside down. And I should spend more time looking at myself. Maybe I can try and not dig my heels in this time. I don't want another lecture. I need to tell my boss what I'm going to do to fix this. I know that I need to stop taking this so personally and taking offense at every negative bit of feedback. I need to remember that when an employee questions a choice I make, he doesn't mean to criticize me. He is probably just trying to help. And I need to figure out a way to engage these people differently.

"I'll tell my boss this . . . From now on, first, I'm going to take a breath and consider what they are saying before I react. Second, I'm going to ask a question to get more information without judging or telling the employees they're wrong. Third, I'm going to spend more time developing a shared vision with my team. They need to feel ownership of the challenge. Lastly, I'm going take some time for myself to vent some of this stress. I've got to rewire my brain and break out of my old mindset because it's holding me back."

What's going on with Brooke?

- She's *seeing* herself clearly. Brooke is getting honest with herself about how people experience working for her. She's cracking open the window enough to let her insecurities surface. Brooke recognizes that she might be her own worst enemy. Being controlling is not the same thing as being a strong, effective leader.
- She's *thinking* with an open mind-set. Brooke is starting to think like a conscious leader. She is examining her assumptions about what it means to be a leader. She has decided to take positive action rather than just complain. She is slowly learning how to be flexible and open to new ideas and stop knee-jerk emotional reactions.
- She's *feeling* comfortable with positive emotions. Brooke is being conscious that her negative emotions are truly hijacking her. Rather than being angry all the time and being driven by her fear of showing weakness or making a mistake, she is consciously shifting her emotions from anger and anxiety to more trust and respect.
- She's *acting* constructively. Brooke is slowly translating her new mind-set into more positive behaviors. By approaching her boss differently, she is inviting her boss into a more cordial mentoring relationship. Her approach to employees will diffuse their defensiveness. Brooke may need to be out on the diving board herself for a while, but practice will give her confidence and her colleagues will see that she wants to change.

It's not enough to do your own work. What is often missing is that you are part of a system that is affecting how you live and work. You are changing all the time inside teams, organizations, and communities. And these systems are influencing you.

Just as we influence the health of a team, the team influences how we behave and perform. Teams have accelerators like clear goals, trust and respect, and open dialogue. We all know too well that teams also have hijackers. These might include unclear roles, too much conflict or politics, or lack of accountability. These team accelerators and hijackers can bring out the best in us or sabotage our best efforts.

Many of us work in organizations that are unhealthy. It's not unusual to go to a leadership workshop only to return to find the boss and the environment contradicting everything we just learned. We must be conscious of how our organizations also have accelerators and hijackers. At Healthy Companies, we find the most common accelerators are inspiring leaders, collaborative teams, and innovative cultures. Common hijackers include toxic managers, bureaucratic silos, and unclear decision-making rights.

The key for you is to be aware of how these larger systems impact your health and performance. The more conscious you are, the easier it is to influence these hijackers and accelerators. But the first step starts with you.

PART V

STEP UP
To Your
Highest Potential

Heading south from Central Park to a meeting at City Hall, the mayor of New York City wasn't expecting the end of the world. It didn't look like a superstorm was about to barrel into the metropolis of 8.5 million. It just looked like another rainy day in autumn 2012. But as Michael Bloomberg stepped into the planning meeting and the sun began to set, things took a turn for the worse in lower Manhattan.

Hurricane Sandy turned out to be Mayor Bloomberg's 9/11 moment. It was a storm of storms, the one that transformed his life and redefined his purpose. Approaching his final year in office, Bloomberg was looking forward to easing into private life and running his brand-new super-PAC. The storm, however, had different plans. The rising tides of Sandy shut down the entire city, flooding the subway and streets along the Hudson River. Its impact was so profound that within days of the hurricane hitting, Bloomberg was moved to speak out about the threat of climate change, saying, "This issue is too important. We need determined leadership at the national level to move the nation and the world forward."[1]

A businessman turned politician, turned social activist, Michael Bloomberg is a man who has been stepping up his entire life. Hurricane Sandy was a very visible moment in his public life as mayor, and he chose to step up and take a position on energy in general and on fossil fuels, particularly coal. Bloomberg saw the problem clearly, telling the UK's *The Guardian,* "Coal is the single biggest polluter. If you could just replace coal with any other fuel, you would make an enormous difference in the outlook for climate change."[2]

So far in this book, "Going Deep" helped us to discover our inner world. "Think Big" explored ways to see a world of possibilities. "Get Real" asked us to examine our accelerators and hijackers. "Step Up" is about leadership and action.

Michael Bloomberg is the personification of stepping up. The owner of one of America's largest private companies, he now focuses on his new endeavor, Bloomberg Philanthropies. Turning his resources and power from making money and building political influence, today he is focused on making the world a better place.

Bloomberg is willing to be bold, principled, and responsible to the larger world. He could choose the luxury of a rich, quiet life. Instead, at a time of unparalleled polarization in the world, he has made it his mission to awaken others to our climate challenges and is unafraid to stand up and take on climate change nay-sayers.[3]

Throughout his life, Bloomberg continually learned how to be courageous and step up. We can too. Many of us approach the world too cautiously, too timidly, too small. We fail to unleash our personal power, which is central to bold leadership. When we step up, we catapult ourselves into a much bigger version of ourselves. If we don't stand up for ourselves, we can never speak our truth. Hiding behind our need for safety, we miss opportunities because we don't take enough risks. That's why in the upcoming chapters, we talk about having the courage to use our power, to challenge others to be good human beings, and to synchronize doing good with reaching our goals.

As we step up, we learn to live our purpose and amplify our senses. This gives us a clearer vision and keener insight, making us more conscious and connected. It also leads to tapping into the voice inside us that challenges the status quo. This is the heart of constructive impatience. It's the part of us that feels responsible to lead people into the future and help them grow and change. Lastly, we need to step up and build our own legacy and contribute to the world.

Like Michael Bloomberg, everyone today must be a transformational leader. Whether a web designer pushing the envelope on design, a sales manager finding new customers in unusual places, a government official streamlining bureaucracy, or a global executive bringing new solutions to Europe, we must all be champions of change.

CHAPTER 21

Live Your Higher Purpose

In the TV show *Blue Bloods,* an Irish-American family in New York City sits down to a ritual dinner every Sunday night. The weekly dinner symbolizes how the family, one side cops, the other side prosecutors, is dedicated to a higher purpose, no matter how much they clash or argue. They represent the American version of noblesse oblige. Here's an old French tradition whereby people with more power and influence are obliged to act in healthy and responsible ways with others as they pursue their goals for success.

Conscious people bring their best selves to the table, and have the courage to challenge others to be good human beings – with their families, work teams, and communities. Like the characters in *Blue Bloods,* living your purpose allows you to merge doing good with achieving your goals whether you are a teacher, a parent, a politician, or a business leader.

An irony of human life is that we all possess a higher purpose, yet many of us have no idea what it is. Our minds and bodies are intended for more than merely survival – they are vessels for deep social and emotional drives that give us meaning. For whatever reason, many people have never asked themselves, "What is my purpose here? Am I meant to do more with my life than take care of myself?"

So how do you discover your higher purpose? By looking at yourself in the mirror and tapping into your innate wisdom and humanity. Your accelerators, like hope, faith, confidence, and optimism, will also help. If you act with higher purpose, things generally turn out better. Your purpose will be your gateway to engagement and motivation and the overarching driver for action. It will give you energy to move forward and free you to make your unique contributions in the world.

Ultimately, purpose is the connection between what we do and why we do it. Indeed, surveys show that three out of four executives report their principal driver in life is the belief that their work has purpose and meaning.[1] It's about being bold and stepping up. If we want to be conscious people, we really need to personify and champion our purpose. So, ask yourself these questions:

- What do I love doing and what am I passionate about?
- When do I feel most alive?
- What are my natural talents and skills?
- What do others say are my special abilities and qualities?
- What values am I most committed to and when do I feel best about myself?
- What would I change in the world if I could?

LEAD WITH YOUR NORTH STAR

Aside from the sun, navigators believe the most important star in the sky is the North Star. It's a humble star, not shining very brightly but always there and reliable. If you find yourself lost on a clear night without a compass, the North Star can be your best friend. Metaphorically, the North Star represents our higher purpose, leading us to take action and make our own lives and the lives of those around us better. But if you are not keeping your purpose consciously close to your mind and heart, it's easy to wander off. Just pick up the daily newspaper and you'll see "successful men and women" who lost their way. It's easy to do in the disruptive and accelerating world.

Conscious leaders are driven by fundamental, undeniable principles. These principles are deeply ingrained in us, shaped over a lifetime of development and introspection. They serve as a moral compass, an internal guidance system that has honesty and fairness as its magnetic north. At its heart is being a grounded and conscious person.

When we are grounded by our principles, we have the courage to be ourselves. We are not afraid of tough issues and stand firm in the face of struggle and adversity. We know we are a mixture of altruism and self-interest, and cannot always be counted on to do the right thing. Still, we know that consistency is better than hypocrisy, and honesty is better than deception. Now, all this sounds nice, but the real test comes when we try to put our principles into action.

To follow your North Star, you need to be vigilant and aware of the changes around you. These are the dilemmas that confront us every day and can sway us off course. At some point, all of us face conflicts between who we are and what we do. This is a wandering moment when you need to engage in an internal conversation about who you want to be in the world. The more conscious you are, the easier it is to remember your purpose and manage through these contradictions.

RIGHT INTENTIONS LEAD TO RIGHT ACTIONS

To bring your purpose alive, you must translate it into deliberate action. Everything starts with your intent – your internal drive to act. Intentions can be positive or negative. Regardless, they influence everything we do. Positive intentions are kindness, service, or excellence. They add value to people's lives. Greed, jealousy, envy, and fear fuel our negative intentions. When people are driven by these ghosts, we are often selfish, spiteful, protective, or detached. The goal is to know the inner truth that drives you.

It's amazing how people can see and feel our intentions even when we believe they are hidden. That's why we need to be aware of our own intent before we act, and check ourselves for any lurking hijackers that can produce unwanted consequences. Sometimes we step up with good intentions and bad things happen – like perfectionists who are motivated to produce a great product, yet their behavior can be interpreted as being too controlling. Compare that to a high-driving boss committed to success. People like to be on a winning team, but they don't like to be told they are wrong all the time.

When you step up to assert yourself, to challenge the status quo, or to change something, you are telling the world that you are taking personal responsibility for your life and actions. So own your intentions, speak your truth, keep agreements, and practice integrity. Your right intentions will lead to right actions.

DON'T GET SEDUCED BY POWER

Let's start with a definition of "power." It's the ability to act to influence others – so, what happens when you turn purpose into action? It gives you power in the world, and that's a good thing. But like most things in life, how we use power can either liberate or sabotage us. We can use power or abuse power. It can be a true catalyst for change or a blocker to progress.

Many of us are afraid of the concept of power. It often conjures up images of autocrats and control freaks like the manipulative lead character Frank Underwood on the Netflix series *House of Cards*. Not to mention how Kevin Spacey abused his power in real life. Not wanting to be known as arrogant, controlling, or too self-interested, we shy away from using our personal power in the world. We hold ourselves back, don't always speak truth to power, and thus, never reach our full potential. Yet, not using our power gets in the way of fulfilling our purpose.

On the flip side, some of us can get seduced by power. We love having control, believe we're better than others, or abuse the power we have. Don't fall trap to this power game. Power can blind, delude, and sabotage. We can overestimate the power we have over people and underestimate the power we have on people. Abuse of power can be seen at our dinner tables, in the hallways of our organizations, and with our friends. Tales of abuse of power are daily fodder for TV news and social media revelations.

Success even has a mysterious way of deluding us into believing our own public relations. Research shows that as people move up in organizations, they believe they are personally responsible for positive results and blame others when things go south.[2] Go figure?

So, speak your mind, stand up for your values, and remember that no one can ever take away who you are as a person. Always remember that as you move up in the world, be true to yourself and be generous in sharing your power. Like anxiety, you only need just enough power to make a difference. When you step up, employ just enough to achieve your purpose without losing sight of your North Star.

Take a bucket of ice water, dump it over your head, challenge others to do it, make a donation, record the whole thing, and post the video on social media. Remember this incredibly successful viral fundraiser? With the ALS Ice Bucket Challenge, Peter Frates figured out how to mobilize millions of people to do the right thing.

Frates was diagnosed with ALS (often referred to as Lou Gehrig's disease) in 2012 at the age of 27. He went quickly from being a professional baseball player to being wheelchair bound and unable to speak. Instead of giving up, Frates stepped up and became the spokesperson for the ALS Association. He noticed the need to raise ALS awareness and research funds to battle the disease. So, he took action. Frates says his disease, rather than crippling him entirely, has led him to find his purpose in life. In 2016, the ALS Association announced that the University of Massachusetts Medical School identified a third gene that is a cause for the disease, crediting donations from the Ice Bucket Challenge, leading to new therapies.[3]

CHAPTER 22

Amplify Your Personal Sensors

Sonar is the best-known maritime sensor. It quietly listens to large swaths of the ocean and navigates through and detects objects on or under the water's surface. This sensitive listening device paints a vivid picture of the invisible world under the sea.

Whether by intention or by osmosis, two of the better listeners in leadership today can be found working at Newport News Shipbuilding. Jennifer Boykin, president, and Lucas Ceballos, a foreman on the deck, have a lot in common. They both mirror the technology they work to create. Newport News Shipbuilding is the world's largest builder of aircraft carriers and submarines, ships that rely heavily on sensors to function.

As leaders, Boykin and Ceballos have learned to function like sonar. They have finely tuned their mental sensors to monitor their environment. Boykin senses how everything in the shipyard fits and works together. Ceballos intuits what each mechanic needs, to win their hearts and minds. Like the sensitive instruments they build, they use their mental senses – listening, intuiting, and experiencing in real time – to become aware of the needs and concerns of their stakeholders.

Boykin leads 20 000 employees, spanning five different generations. As a child who grew up in an integrated neighborhood, she learned how to intuitively tailor her messages and tap the energy of diverse people. By activating her personal sensors, she learns what's important, what unique skills people bring, and how to motivate them. Says Boykin, "Our leaders at all levels need to know how to use their sensors – to listen to people's concerns, make the right improvements, and on any given day, make sure we are on the right track." Jennifer is aware of her environment – understanding every step of the shipbuilding process.[1]

Ceballos is the foreman for new submarine construction projects and leads the mechanics who build the submarine's propeller shaft. He shares Boykin's ability to activate his personal sensors, listening deeply to what is going on around him. Believing that everyone is a leader, he sees his main role as sensing people; moving them forward in the company; and being there to support, trust, and respect them in any way he can. His advice: "If you're not there for your people, then they're not going to be there for you. Expect what you put out."[2]

LISTEN DEEPLY

Since the world is moving so fast, we must activate and amplify our senses. Not just our five senses – seeing, hearing, smelling, touching, and tasting. We also need to put our mental senses – our "mental sonar" to work – listening, intuiting, feeling, and experiencing in real time. Our mental sonar lets us put our relationship awareness into action.

Most of us don't listen well. We learn to listen like we speak. We are too preoccupied with where we are going. We spend too much time thinking about how to respond to or one-up the person talking to us. By being a good listener, we make a conscious choice to open our ears and stop talking so much.

Conscious people listen well. They swipe away backstories and use a clean mental slate, not biases, to listen, learn, and deepen understanding. They ask more questions and make fewer declarations. They walk in other people's shoes to find fresh ways to solve problems. Their intuition is their greatest tool.

Empathy is their secret weapon. Newport News Shipbuilding's Ceballos shares an early leadership story that taught him well. One day he asked an older mechanic, "How are you doing?" The mechanic replied, "No one's ever asked me much about my well-being." The employee had recently lost his wife, and as a new leader, Ceballos didn't quite know how to handle the situation. So, he relied on his personal sensors. He listened with an emotional ear to the mechanic, sharing that he had lost his own father recently. A wonderful conversation ensued. By expressing his empathy and compassion, a deeper relationship was born and the workplace was made to feel a little more human that day for both the foreman and the mechanic.

GET TO KNOW YOUR STAKEHOLDERS

Listening from the inside out is critical, for sure. Yet we must also listen from the outside in. In our 24/7 world, connections are everywhere, and the world shows up every moment we turn on our cell phones. The more aware we are of the outside world, the more we can navigate through change. That is why conscious people understand relationships and the environments in which they live and work.

For starters, conscious people have a very distinct way of viewing their social spaces. They see their families, organizations, and communities as places of value, and places to create value. The reciprocity of giving and getting is their golden rule. By growing trusted relationships, we learn faster, move farther, and adapt more quickly.

So, create value for yourself by making friends with your stakeholders. A stakeholder is anyone in your life with an interest or concern in you. Your spouse is a primary stakeholder; so is your boss. Your customers are, both inside and outside of work. Your friends are stakeholders; so is your daughter's Montessori teacher. The CEO of your company is; so are your suppliers. If you're going to be a conscious person, you need to know how your stakeholders think and feel. You need to actively sense what they need and want from you, just as much as you need to tell them what you need and want from them. Part of your job is making life easier for your stakeholders.

You also need to listen to how the world works. What are the external forces affecting you and your company? What's the impact of current events on your work and life? How are the trends in business and government influencing you? Are you creating value for your organization? Are your stakeholders feeling understood and valued? By staying aware of your environment, you will be one step ahead of your peers.

LEVEL YOUR TRIPOD

A tripod is a handy tool to explain life's balancing act. Kick out one of the legs and your camera ends up on the ground. Same applies to our lives. One leg is our work life, another is our family life, and the third leg is our personal life. Our personal sensors need to be fine-tuned to all three to keep us healthy and balanced.

Think about your typical day. You arrive to work early to get a jump on your e-mails. Soon people begin to show up at your office with problems and issues that need your immediate input. Next, it's back-to-back meetings where you stay focused for a couple of hours, concentrating on what everyone needs and says. Your energy may flag because of jet lag, a bad night's sleep, or having spent some of the previous night on the phone dealing with an overseas crisis. To pump yourself up, you take a mental break, drink a couple cups of coffee, or go for a short walk.

Lunch is quick and at your desk, but you avoid heavy foods that slow you down. During the afternoon, you're on your feet visiting departments and checking on projects while juggling phone calls. At the end of the afternoon, you're back in your office to go over budget figures with your CFO. It's early evening before you get to go home, no gym today, spend some fast "quality time" with your kids, and off to bed after a quick recap of the day with your spouse.

Impressive just to think about – all the energy you marshal to propel yourself both mentally and physically through the myriad demands of being a leader. Energy to handle long days, energy to mentally juggle priorities and tasks, energy to concentrate and think clearly, energy to manage people's personal issues, energy to focus on your children, and finally energy to negotiate with your partner about tomorrow's tasks.

If the above sounds like you, your focus is primarily on your work life. The other two legs – personal and family – are likely being neglected. Making sure all three legs are sturdy is critical to living a healthy and productive life. It's inevitable that one of these legs will become vulnerable from time to time – during work stress, marital difficulties, challenges with kids, or health problems. Then it's time to rely on the other legs to keep us sturdy and resilient.

Being conscious and aware of this balancing act will alert you to the risk for burnout. When Sunday comes around and your son wants to play soccer, your husband wants to play golf, your daughter needs a ride to dance class, and you want to visit with friends, maybe it's the time to level the tripod to make sure you leave time for yourself. Step up, scan your environment, turn on your mental sonar, and remember it's time to balance the tripod.

So, how do you amplify your sensors? Are you listening deeply to what's going on inside and around you? How well are you listening to your stakeholders? Are you operating with a level tripod?

Maybe it's time to become more conscious of your external environment. You have many personal sensors at your disposal. By quietly listening to people and your surroundings, you will sense what is important and create the outcomes you most desire. You'll be amazed how conscious awareness and deliberate action work together.

CHAPTER 23

Lead with Constructive Impatience

In the pantheon of great living leaders, you will always find Germany's Angela Merkel and Amazon's Jeff Bezos. What do these two powerhouses have in common? They both lead with constructive impatience. Merkel leans toward constructive and Bezos leans toward impatience. But both know how to engage people and get things done, making it safe while challenging the limits, being constructive in approach, while being impatient to reach desired outcomes.

Raised behind the Iron Curtain, Merkel first appeared in the West as a divorced 35-year-old East German physicist specializing in quantum chemistry. Her scientific lens empowers her to make sense of seeming randomness in human systems. As the German chancellor governing over 87 million people, Merkel sees solutions where most people see confusion. This allows her to challenge people, in her constructive way, to higher levels of performance. Merkel knows how to bring out the best in others. As a result, her power and influence have steadily grown within the European Union and around the world. Yet, she's not afraid to show her impatience either, whether she is pushing Germans to rethink the refugee crisis or making it clear that there is no place for walls, nation-states, fascism, or totalitarianism in Europe.[1]

Jeff Bezos enjoys more high-velocity decision making. Amazon was launched in 1994. Today, he oversees 150,000 people and $90 billion in revenue. In his 2016 letter to shareholders, he explains his rationale for constructive impatience: "Most decisions should probably be made with somewhere around 70% of the information you wish you had. If you wait for 90%, in most cases, you're probably being too slow."[2] With speed in mind, Bezos has built the world's largest online superstore and has branched out to include affiliates, platforms, cloud services, film studios, and his recent acquisition of Whole Foods supermarkets. It's a strategy obsessed with customers and growth that applies just enough pressure to push the limits, sometimes more.

We live in an age of accelerations. This puts pressure on all of us to step up, to raise the bar on ourselves and our institutions. People are challenged to expand their minds. Organizations are pressured to improve their performance. Merkel and Bezos know this instinctively. They share a deep understanding that complacency or chaos are the enemies of progress and growth. That's why they lead with constructive impatience.

IT ALL STARTS AT HOME

If you want others to step up, you had better start with yourself. This is the heart of constructive impatience. It's the voice inside you that challenges the status quo. It's your courage to take risks, to travel into the unknown, to desire something better. It's the part of you that feels responsible to lead people into the future. Whether you're an executive, coach, or parent, it's about challenging others to be bigger and better tomorrow than they are today.

Conscious people understand that any change must start with them. Leaders like Merkel and Bezos, and millions of others, have personal conversations like these every day. By becoming more conscious, we learn to be our own personal agents of change. Only then can we challenge others to step up.

Some of us tend to be constructive by nature, building psychologically safe environments for ourselves. Others of us are naturally impatient, challenging our limits, pushing ourselves to expand capabilities beyond what we imagined. Chances are you lean toward one side of this paradox or the other, especially when you are under pressure. But the paradox, constructive impatience, has two parts inextricably bound together to create positive energy and results. Too much focus on constructive energy spawn complacency; too much impatience breeds unnecessary errors. So, where do you stand on this continuum?

BEING CONSTRUCTIVE

When leading others, being constructive is at the top of the list. It's about creating a psychologically safe environment built on trust and respect. This is a compassionate approach to leadership. People feel good about themselves. Their work has meaning. They feel valued and appreciated. They stretch beyond their current image of themselves and are more agile and willing to change. If you can achieve this, people will be better team players and more willing to challenge themselves to higher levels of performance.

Conscious people are masters at creating sane environments. Since they understand being safe and sane inside themselves, it's easy for them to build deep connections with others. Instead of creating islands of self-interest, they emphasize collaboration and community.

What does being constructive look like? You might consider:

- Focusing on the best in people.
- Developing a positive employee experience.
- Pushing decisions as far down as possible.
- Helping people find meaning in their work.
- Turning mistakes into lessons.
- Sharing yourself authentically.

Now, some people have trouble being constructive. It goes against their nature. They live a life of constant challenge or mistrust. They may have been taught early on that being too nice is a sign of weakness. They may see collaboration as a waste of time. Or they may just think that safety buys mediocrity. To them, people need fear to be motivated. There's simply too much to do to worry about how people feel.

At the other extreme are those who go overboard on being constructive. These are people generally afraid of their own feelings and the feelings of others. Under the guise of protecting people, they are really trying to protect themselves. They will do just about anything to avoid confrontation. By overrelying on consensus, they smother conflict and creative spirit, resulting in analysis paralysis. While there are many obstacles to creating a constructive work environment, none is more insidious than complacency.

If you're struggling with being constructive, your hijackers are likely to be the culprit. Check yourself for the following: Are you overly cautious, fearful of pushing too hard, or overpleasing to be liked? You can fend off your hijackers by tapping into your accelerators, like being more courageous, allowing yourself to be vulnerable, and driving through your resistance.

BEING IMPATIENT

Jeff Bezos was impatient from the early start-up days at Amazon. What he envisioned was a company on the edge, always putting the customer first. Here's an interesting tidbit. He registered the domain name Relentless.com before landing on the name Amazon. Even today, Relentless.com redirects you to Amazon.[3] What Bezos has mastered is his ability to tap into a deep human desire. Everybody wants to make a contribution. This requires a sense of urgency, a need for action, a hunger to improve. People with this skill know how to use impatience to step up.

If you are a naturally impatient person, like Jeff Bezos, setting bold goals, challenging limits, and pushing yourself to do bigger and better things is built into your psychological makeup. When you lead others, you tap into their inborn desire to win, push people out of their comfort zones, and look for opportunities to raise the bar on performance.

Warning: Impatience can be toxic. Push too hard and you become a bully. Be overly aggressive, and you alienate others. Be impulsive or reckless, and others lose trust in you. Don't run the risk of going overboard and becoming careless. Being conscious and aware of others will prevent these mishaps.

Again, this is where knowing your hijackers can help. If you struggle with being too impatient, take a closer look at your perfectionism, critical demeanor, obsession with success, or stress and burnout. You'll likely find the culprit there.

Constructive impatient leaders challenge people to perform in a safe environment. They balance setting stretch goals with getting buy-in. They know when to push hard and when to let things happen naturally. They balance compassion with a drive for results. They know people do their best work when they are respected and stretched.

Here are some tips to consider:

- Always look for opportunities to improve.
- Set sky-high goals with incremental touch points.
- Push people to do better than they imagine.
- Live in the future and the present simultaneously.
- Tie your success to the success of others.
- Give people what they need to succeed.

How constructive and impatient are you? Are you comfortable living in the gap, the paradox of being ambitious *and* grateful? Do you stretch people *and* embrace people? Are you inclined to change things *and* stay the course if it's working? Are you able to move fast *and* go slow? Essentially you are being asked to add one plus one and make it equal three – in other words, to live and lead with constructive impatience. This is the fuel for great execution.

CHAPTER 24

Make Civility Your Guide

Have you ever experienced road rage? Got caught in the crossfire of a Twitter war? Lost a friend over a Facebook post? Or been berated by a colleague? You are not alone. The annual report *Civility in America*, a multiyear survey by public relations firm Weber Shandwick, shows that there is a major problem in the way we treat each other.[1] Has the sun set on civility? Has everyone forgotten the Golden Rule?

In the midst of a civility crisis, the only way out is to make civility your guide. The essence of civility, being conscious about being courteous and considerate, is the foundation of all relationships. Civility lets you disagree without disrespect, find a starting point for dialogue, and distance yourself from biases. Understanding the humanity and diversity of others lies at the heart of civility. Being more conscious solves our incivility problems.

So, what is incivility? Behaviors that belittle, demean, insult, bully, or rudely dismiss others. Many of us know incivility is wrong, but we don't do anything about it. Yet, incivility is contagious and poisons relationships inside families and teams. When people work under a cloud of negativity, they stop taking risks, make more mistakes, and fail to collaborate. Managers end up spending more time mending uncivil behavior. Team spirit deteriorates and customers get alienated by what they see. Mistrust and cynicism control the environment.

There is deep truth in the axiom "You get what you give," especially in the wild, wireless world. No CEO has experienced this to the degree Neal Patterson did. As founder and CEO of a software firm, Patterson found himself displeased with employee performance and decided to take action. Via e-mail he proceeded to bully and demean employees. Essentially, he lost it for a few moments and hit the "send" button.

Patterson didn't understand the power of civility. His lapse of emotional control showed up on Yahoo! within days of an employee posting it. It was seen by millions of people. For Patterson, the cost of incivility had a number attached to it: He watched the market cap of his company drop $300 million and his personal wealth shrink by $28 million.[2]

It's easy to find horror stories born of incivility. You probably have personal experience with a few. On the other hand, it's a lot harder to find a heroic story that comes from people acting with civility. They are just good people. In our society, that doesn't make headlines. Take, for example, Mark Gensheimer. He's one of the good guys you wouldn't hear about.

Gensheimer is the president of CS McKee, an institutional money management firm. As a leader, he understands there is a market for civility. He learned this from his parents and his mentally disabled younger brother, who helped Gensheimer appreciate the value of respect. A true believer in the goodness of everyone, he walks the talk of civility at work and life. Says Mark, "I've always had a natural interest in getting to know people. You just need to peel back the onion a little bit before you see the goodness. And it just amazes me, when you ask people a little bit about their history you find a human connection with them."[3]

Today, "Gensch," as his friends fondly call him, is surrounded by wonderful women in his life, his wife of 34 years and four wonderful daughters. One wonders whether that had something to do with it, too. Confident and humble, positive and playful, Gensheimer sheds light on his big network of family, friends, and colleagues. He reflects, "I try to help people feel comfortable in their own skin. When that happens, people enjoy life and perform better and that's a good thing."[3]

Conscious people realize there is a human being on the other end of every connection. Acts of civility are the small sacrifices we make for the good of all and the sake of harmoniously living and working together. By being civil to others, you show mutual respect, appreciation, and fairness. Conscious is the Golden Rule.

BECOME A MATURE ADULT

Many of us get dragged kicking and screaming into adulthood. Often, a degree of arrested development follows us through college and into our early work years. It's not easy to grow up and become evolved adults. We are vulnerable to being hijacked by people and situations that push our buttons. Relationships are messy, and no one said life was easy. But if we want to live in a civil society, we need to regularly turn the mirror and ask ourselves, "Do I have the courage to take the high road? What's so wrong with admitting mistakes, being generous, or saying, 'I'm sorry'?"

It's not to say you can't be playful or foolish, competitive or opinionated. Being a mature adult means having the ability to see the bigger picture and reprioritize personal needs and self-interests to play on the team. Maturity is about being a fully developed person with all your imperfections.

Blaming politicians, the Internet, or reality TV for our growing incivility is a dangerous game to play. Ignoring the people around you also compounds the civility problem. Tuning out is not an option. The real buck stops with you. Awakening our courage to be civil is nonnegotiable in our polarizing world. Conscious people stay present and lead the way.

BALANCE SELFISHNESS AND SELFLESSNESS

Every airline instructs passengers that in the event of an emergency, oxygen masks will drop from the ceiling. They explicitly tell parents to always put their own mask on before helping their children. Here's the reason: Selfishness is the necessity of taking care of yourself so you can help others. You need to be selfish to be selfless.

Selfishness is based on our survival instincts. The ability to put oneself first is ingrained in who we are. It shows up in our desire to succeed, and our need to protect ourselves from hurtful criticism and vulnerable situations. Focusing on ourselves keeps attention on the one person we have a responsibility to control.

Selflessness is the art of taking care of others to the extent that it does not harm you. It's all about balance, being reasonable, and exhibiting self-control. Too much selflessness feels "holier than thou," competing to be the most altruistic person in the room. Too much selfishness makes you uncaring and unempathetic.

So, when it comes to being civil, we need a "both/and" solution that values our self-interests and our common interests, our desire to be a good person and our need to take care of ourselves.

If we look deep inside ourselves, we have the solution to being more civil. Just be more conscious. It empowers us to step up and be the person we want to see in others. Empathy begets empathy, trust begets trust, candor begets candor, caring begets caring. The more civil we are with others, the more civil they will be with us.

SHARE GRATITUDE AND GENEROSITY

Gratitude is the lifeblood of our spiritual health. In its simplest form, it's saying "thank you." When we show appreciation to ourselves and others, we are saying we care. In a world of scarcity and competition, gratitude is the real expression of compassionate leadership. It's civility in practice.

Many of us don't appreciate ourselves. Why prioritize loving yourself first? But, if we don't give ourselves permission to be human, if we don't stroke ourselves for a job well done, we will never be free to fully appreciate others.

TIPS FOR CONSCIOUS LIVING

Assess yourself.

- Take a moment to simply stop and reflect on what you are grateful for in your life. Why? And how does it make your life better? Keep a gratitude journal. Some people find it important to ask this question every day to remind themselves that the cup is half full, not half empty.

Practice the Golden Rule.

- Do unto others as you wish they would do unto you. Ask people what excites and motivates them, show appreciation publicly, give negative feedback privately, give without expecting in return, and honor people with your full attention.

How do you relate?

- Be conscious of how you relate to others. Regularly ask yourself about the impact of your behavior on others. Tell those you care about how grateful you are to have them in your life. Not only will you feel better, but you will also brighten their day.

Commit to being civil every day.

- Be kind and loving. Write a personal note of appreciation. Look someone in the eye and smile. Catch people in the act of doing something right. Words and actions matter. They turn ill will to good will.

Create a civility code at work.

- There are simple ways to foster and demand civility at work. Calling out civility is a good place to start. Avoid situations that generate negative energy, like failing to return phone calls or e-mails, ignoring others, not keeping appointments, or being publicly dismissive of people.

When it comes to appreciation, some of us are simply scared. We think it might open up Pandora's box; people might stop working hard or misinterpret our good wishes. However, this thinking is wrong. Expressing gratitude creates an atmosphere of loyalty and engagement. A study by Bersin at Deloitte examined companies known for their strong expression of appreciation. The appreciative companies were 12 times more likely to show better results than companies less generous.[4]

Showing gratitude and generosity is not just about money or material gifts. In truth, gratitude is much more personal than that. It's about giving praise, or giving up some control and offering more responsibility. When you are grateful, you are likely to feel happier and more at peace with yourself.

CHAPTER 25

Build a Shared Consciousness

All living things are interconnected through networks of relationships. We depend on this web of life to survive.

—Thomas Friedman, New York Times *best-selling author*[1]

What makes humans stand out is our capacity to be aware of our connections. True connectedness is based on shared consciousness – a belief that we need one another to excel, and are stronger together than apart.

We all have a yearning for belonging. Being part of a community makes us feel good. We are simply happier and more productive when we are part of a group. So, we must rely on each other to be conscious.

Here's the dilemma. In today's fast-paced, digitally connected world, we are struggling emotionally in a crisis of disconnection. Polarization, partisanship, and loneliness are commonplace. Brené Brown, in *Braving the Wilderness,* believes we are cutting ourselves off from real connection with other people. This is due to fear – fear of vulnerability, fear of hurt and pain, and fear of criticism and conflict. Says Brown, "We want to be part of something yet we are standing alone in the wilderness."[2]

Sitting in the shadow of Silicon Valley, Stanford Healthcare is as high-tech as you would expect. Grissel Hernandez, a nursing professional development specialist at Stanford, noticed that this access to cutting-edge technology brought with it both a blessing and a curse. "One of the challenges that nurses face is to balance the need to save someone's life with all the technology that you can possibly throw at them, never forgetting there's a human being behind the curtain."

A negative side effect of high-tech health care is that nursing is faster, more complex, and carries more pressure to do more with less. What it has gained in efficiency it has lost in depersonalization. Patients become tasks instead of human beings. Hernandez was challenged with helping her nursing staff be more authentic while using the technology tools.

Grissel found a low-tech solution. She turned to the remarkably mundane micro-practice of hand washing, and transformed it into an effective exercise in self-care that her nurses use 5 to 30 times a shift. Rather than mentally checking out during each 30-second hand washing, she asks nurses to take a deep breath, recite a mantra, or say a prayer. Hernandez helps them use the moment to take care of themselves. "It's amazing when you bring consciousness back to the work. It moves you away from that automated, auto-pilot way of caring for people, and it brings you back to the true purpose of nursing."[3]

Hernandez's micro-practice is a good example of how to strengthen the shared consciousness of people at work. In the complicated, life-and-death nature of nursing, her low-tech solution solved a complex human problem.

Every workplace has its hand-washing moments – ritual times to pause, promote well-being, celebrate the shared mission, and deepen connections and awareness. It's the leader's job to find and exploit these moments for the good of the workplace. At Stanford Healthcare, Grissel Hernandez is dedicated not only to saving lives but to saving nurses too.

There are three essential behaviors needed to build shared consciousness: Show up and be real, make and keep commitments, and make "we" your highest priority.

SHOW UP AND BE REAL

Angela Ahrendts, Apple's senior vice president of retail and online sales, arises before 5 a.m. not to work or swim laps. Instead, she spends a half hour watching the sun rise or reading her favorite passage from Maya Angelou. Without this time for reflection, she has repeatedly said, she would not be the leader she is today. "The world is moving fast. Unless I come into the office in the morning and smile, walk in the lobby and say, 'good morning!' – if I am stressed – I am not going to do a good job."[4]

As leaders, everyone is watching us. Our emotions are contagious. We energize and de-energize people. Leadership is truly a connection, an opportunity to tap into the heads and hearts of people. To build a shared purpose, mutual trust, and a sense of community. To involve people deeply in the process. To tap into the collective intelligence of the group.

Showing up involves the obvious: Your physical presence, body language, tone of voice, what you say and do. It also means being mentally present and invested in others and what is going on around you. Being your real self means you share your thoughts and feelings, and you have the courage to expose yourself psychologically.

By telling the truth to yourself, you learn to be emotionally honest with others. Remember, the key to our intelligence is not inside our own minds, but inside the minds of the people around us. So, don't be afraid to speak up when others are avoiding the tough issues. Be direct and authentic. Both you and they will be better leaders, colleagues, and human beings.

Nothing builds a shared consciousness more than sharing yourself and the business. Sharing information increases trust and accountability. If people had better relationships with their leaders, and more numbers about the business, they would contribute more to productivity.

MAKE AND KEEP COMMITMENTS

People are hungry to be led by real people – leaders who are comfortable in their own skin. But it's the trust between people that holds everything together. Trust is the cornerstone for every great family, team, and organization. Unfortunately, trust is fragile and lost in a moment's thoughtlessness. So, making and keeping commitments is the currency with which we build shared consciousness.

It starts with being clear about your expectations and then, like with any good golf swing, ends with the follow-through. So, what does this entail?

- **Be credible.** Make your written and spoken words believable. Ensure your actions are consistent with your words. When you interact with distrustful people, do the extra work to prove yourself credible. One sure way of losing credibility is to tell lies or half-truths. Better to say nothing or admit you don't know or cannot say than to spin a web of mistruths. That will come back to haunt you.
- **Be dependable.** Deliver on your promises and commitments. Your word is your bond, even in the most difficult or trying situations. People expect leaders to be dependable and mature – to demonstrate a reliable presence. If you don't (and sometimes it's not possible), others are less likely to trust who you really are.
- **Be predictable.** Make sure your train runs on time. This is expressed in your values and temperament. The predictable person does not spring unpleasant surprises on people, does not engage in emotional outbursts, and does not constantly change their positions or opinions without explanation or conversation. Those behaviors undermine people's sense of safety and trust.
- **Be emotionally safe.** Do not abuse people's health, feelings, self-image, or principles. Take their concerns and interests to heart. People who feel emotionally safe know they will not be humiliated or criticized unfairly out of proportion to the situation. Stay mentally focused in conversations. Put aside devices while in meetings and glue your attention to people's faces, not your e-mail inbox.

If you practice this personal honor code, you can avoid the heartaches and headaches of broken promises and neglected commitments. As a leader, you will build trust and credibility when you build shared consciousness.

MAKE "WE" YOUR HIGHEST PRIORITY

Duo Amal ("Amal" means "hope" in Arabic) is a story of "we." Two young, 20-something musicians, Yaron Kohlberg from Israel and Bishari Haroni from Palestine, came together to form a dynamic piano concerto duo. Transcending political and national differences, they believe their music can be a role model and help solve their countries long-standing tensions. They live in a world of "we," and inspire us with hope for a better future. This musical duo demonstrates the power of connection and collaboration.[5]

Did you know that people who use the word "I" more than "we" are at a higher risk of heart attack? They are more self-absorbed and self-centered, and they struggle to put themselves in other people's shoes. This approach to leadership and life causes increased rust in your arteries and alienates friends, employees, and customers alike.[6]

Our accelerating world is quickly leaving the big "I" behind. Research on connections shows that people with larger and more diversified personal networks are higher performers; they get promoted earlier and are considered better leaders.[7] They are successful because of their ability to energize people and attract high performers, raising the performance of the entire group.

Companies with shared consciousness outperform their competitors, too. They create more knowledge, promote innovation, and build more alliances and partnerships. Organizations of tomorrow will be concentric circles of interconnected relationships. Shared consciousness will be the glue that holds the community together.

Finally, let us leave you with a touching story of the "Immortal Fans Campaign of Brazil's Sport Club Recife." It's a story of shared consciousness making the world a better place.

According to Brazilian law, the family of a deceased loved one decides whether their organs will be donated. Making these decisions is not easy in any culture, and in Brazil there was a notoriously large refusal rate for organ donation. Recife's soccer team decided to take action, and to use its power for the greater good.

Brazilian football – or soccer, as it is called in the United States – is known for its hardcore fans. The Recife team made an appeal to the city. The ask was to donate their organs after they die so that their love for the club can live on in someone else's body. Recife's fans and supporters were featured awaiting transplants of corneas, lungs, and hearts from organ donors.

The campaign worked! It helped solve one of the biggest barriers of organ donation in Brazil. Organ donation in Brazil increased by 54% in a year. The campaign is now saving lives and deepening the shared consciousness of the community.[8]

CHAPTER 26

Help Your Garden Grow

In the jungle, life is wild, chaotic, and out of control. In a garden, everything has a purpose. You can build strong roots, weed out bad company, and attend to your buds and flowers. Becoming more conscious lets you see the full circle of life from seeding, to growing, to harvesting. If you think of leadership like your garden, you discover others' gifts, create the right conditions for growth, and remove obstacles along the way. This is how you nourish the leadership in others. This is how to make your garden grow.

Growing gardens is the work of Soma Stout, MD. As the executive leader of the 100 Million Healthier Lives Project, her job is to develop leaders from all walks of life. Stout has a plethora of awards and degrees for her efforts, which are committed to helping solve health care's intractable problem of underserved communities around the world.

Stout's approach is deeply rooted in her childhood and family experiences in India: "I grew up as somebody who came from a family that made $10 a month. In the streets and shantytowns without electricity in Kolkata, I saw all around me people who had enormous gifts, talents and capacities that were often un-utilized or under-utilized, because no one thought to actually ask them." Her childhood observations led her to uncover a sustainable solution: People closer to the problem are more likely to have the knowledge and solutions to address their own challenges. Those are the people who need to become leaders. Those are the people to help grow their own gardens.

One example took place in Guyana. Local health workers, villagers, and teachers with no more than a fifth-grade education had brilliant ideas about how to improve health. When community members took over the development process, malaria rates decreased by 90% and malnutrition was eliminated among widows.

Stout's advocacy for growing leaders and her distributive leadership approach is her trademark. Her advice to grow your garden: "Unlock your potential to learn and grow, and then unlock the potential of others."[1]

NOURISH YOURSELF EVERY DAY

Each of us has the capacity to learn. It's a powerful psychological force that begins early in life and retains itself deep into old age. Our need for self-improvement fuels a special quality that we cannot function without – our autonomy. This is a fierce drive to define ourselves as individuals and determine the course of our lives. It is the propellant that pushes us to conquer the unknown, and to master not just our fate but the world around us.

It may surprise you that we are learning every moment of every day, even while we sleep. In fact, our minds are most active at night – linking the day's activities with memories and habits, creating new insights from the day before, and emerging smarter, more creative, and more conscious.

Here's the interesting challenge. At a time when we must be learning and unlearning as fast as possible, adults of working age (30 to 50) are the most resistant to change. Priorities like getting ahead, raising a family, and generating money often take precedence over development. Pressures to perform and a shortage of time hobble adult learning. Since most jobs require us to take responsibility for our own learning, this is a problem. Today, job tenure is a little more than four years. Job hopping is the new normal. Millennials can expect to have 15 to 20 jobs during their working lives. We simply need more adult learners.

To satisfy our drive for self-improvement, and to stay relevant, we must step up and be curious. Now, we all have special gifts; we may not see them, accept them, or appreciate them. But to be fully alive, we must discover them. Sometimes that happens in unexpected ways.

Brian Cornell has been leading companies for more than 30 years, taking him into the executive suites at Safeway, Michaels Stores, PepsiCo, and Sam's Club. Today he is the chief executive officer of Target. He knows firsthand the benefits of dedicating himself to learning. Part of the process is being comfortable as a teacher and a student.

Cornell shared a life story with us: "Leaders that mature recognize that they can't be perfect. I was criticized for it, wanting to be perfect at an early stage in my career. I wanted to make sure I was completely buttoned up. And my old boss sat me down one day and said, 'Brian, you do great work, you have an amazing work ethic, and you're always organized. Everything is perfect and every word's been thought out. But you should spend more time just being yourself, being genuine, and staying approachable.'"[2]

PLANT GOLDEN SEEDS

Charles Handy, one of the world's most influential management thinkers, knows how to stretch. Speaking to a crowd of developing leaders in London, he shared his advice recently: "To plant a golden seed is to identify a talent in someone – something they're good at – and to point that out to them. If they trust you, it can give them the confidence to go and achieve something with it. High-achievers were almost all given a golden seed in the first 20 years of their lives… So, go forth and plant golden seeds!"[3]

Conscious leaders are good teachers. They understand that most people have an inherent desire to learn and grow. When we invest in ourselves, we can help others find their hidden abilities. We are generous with our time, knowledge, and relationships. This is at the heart of planting golden seeds.

Consider these ideas for developing others:

- Take a personal interest in the people around you – in their goals, fears, and frustrations. You will be amazed by the impact of your green thumb.
- Tap into people's strengths, and help them see their cup as half full and always refillable.
- Give them permission to be vulnerable – allow them to take risks, not have all the answers, make mistakes, and feel the anxiety of change.
- Teach them confidence. Help them see that they are bigger than their image of themselves.
- Share stories about your personal lessons of leadership. Talk about someone who believed in you and tapped your potential.
- Help them learn lessons about setbacks and failures. Maybe it's their perfectionism, fear of failure, or lack of confidence that's tripping them up.
- Reflect on who you have planted a golden seed in within the last 12 months. Write down three names of people in whom you will plant a gold seed in the next 3 months.

INSPIRE AND ENERGIZE OTHERS

The consulting firm Bain & Company surveyed executives from companies all around the world. They asked them about the relationship between satisfaction, engagement, and inspiration, and the impact on productivity. What they found may not surprise you. Inspired people were by far the most productive. They got their meaning and energy from their company's mission and their leaders.[4]

Conscious leaders are inspiring coaches. Whether you are positive or negative, conscious or unconscious, you are modeling behavior for the people who work with you. People naturally look to you for direction. Yet, people also want to know you as a person. They love to peek into your world and guess what you are thinking, what you are planning, and what is important to you. They talk and speculate about you all the time. Why not have as much impact and influence as possible?

Some of your colleagues will be excited to learn from you, and even thank you. Others will never admit their appreciation, or will even resist your coaching because of their need to demonstrate competence or control. Whatever the situation, just remember that you are touching people, whether you like it or not.

In a cynical world, inspiring others may be your ticket to success. People are hungry for coaches to help them navigate through the wilderness of change. So ask yourself: Is your garden growing? Do people feel inspired by you? Are you leaving them bigger and better than you found them? Tilling your garden may be your greatest investment.

CHAPTER 27

Leave a Legacy

At the National Arboretum in Washington, DC, there is a 400-year-old bonsai tree. What's remarkable about this tree is not its age, nor its beauty. What is incredible about the tree is its legacy. Every day since 1625, someone has lovingly cared for this tree, watering and pruning it, regardless of the hardships it encountered. In Japan, the Yamaki family cared for the tree for six generations in the bonsai nursery at their home.

On August 6, 1945, the 320-year-old white oak was sitting in the shade of its garden wall when the world changed forever. An American bomber, the *Enola Gay,* dropped an atomic bomb, scorching the earth of Hiroshima and killing hundreds of thousands. The bonsai only escaped obliteration as the garden wall blocked the atomic flash and the following shockwave. A member of the family saved it from the ensuing firestorm that engulfed the city.[1]

In 1976, the tree was given to the United States as a gift from Japan to celebrate America's bicentennial. At the time, the history of the tree was unknown. Four years later, the bonsai master, Masaru Yamaki, the donor of the tree, unexpectedly paid a visit. At a point in the visit to the National Arboretum, the curator became concerned and uneasy.

As Yamaki was looking at the tree, he became emotional and began to tear. Worried that they were not properly caring for the tree, the curator asked him, through a translator, "Is everything okay?" Yamaki paused a moment, collected himself, and responded, "Yes, the tree is happy here." It wasn't until 2001, when his grandsons visited, that the full history of the bonsai was revealed.[2]

It's difficult to hear this story and not get emotional. It took generations to nurture and grow this bonsai. Those who protected the tree are nameless, yet their legacy lives on in the tree, which has become a symbol of peace and resilience.

This story teaches us that legacy is not vainglorious. Legacy is not all about being remembered or even recognized. History didn't record who cared for this tree over the past four centuries. Yet the passion and dedication of those people show up in every leaf and root of the tree today.

At Healthy Companies, when we work with leaders, one of the first questions we ask is: "What do you want your legacy to be?" It is often a startling question. Most people give it next to no thought. And when they do think of legacy, it's often in the wrong way. They think of legacy as an altruistic celebration of self rather than what it could be, a positive contribution to the world. The Hiroshima bonsai tree is the embodiment of the type of pure legacy we should all strive to build.

We hope our life matters. It's only human to want to be remembered and recognized. Legacy evokes pride, joy, a sense of accomplishment, and purpose. Our meaning comes from working toward something and giving something away. Only you can author your life and be your own human story.

Yet we need to remember that we are building a legacy by every choice we make. Ours is not a legacy in waiting, it's a work in progress. Conscious people see life in context and know what's important. They are leaving a legacy in every moment, every interaction, every day, to actively create a new and better world.

Very few of us get the chance to leave footprints on the moon or build a pyramid or create a company like Apple. Yet all of us can create a legacy that is just as meaningful. The real treasures we leave behind are when we take a new job, build a great team, mentor a colleague, care for an aging parent, or volunteer in the community. It's the ethical choices we make, the artistic creations we produce, and the little acts we perform to protect the environment.

Conscious people deeply understand this. They know they can shape how the world sees them today and how they might be remembered tomorrow. Your legacy can be short-lived or far-reaching – personally, with family and friends and across generations; professionally, with colleagues and even entire industries; and within your community and the greater world. It's up to you to carve your legacy not in stone but in the hearts and minds of the people you have touched.

Remember that the first person in 1625 to care for the Hiroshima bonsai could never have imagined its significance four hundred years and half a world away. They just did what they knew was right: Water the plant, prune the leaves, and love the tree.

It has been a true pleasure spending this time with you. We hope by now you appreciate the full possibilities of being conscious. We wish you the best of luck on your journey. Stay in touch. We are all in this together.

Notes & Further Reading

Chapter 1: The Wild, Wireless World

1. Asher, Claire. "Chameleon Has One of the Fastest Tongues in the Animal Kingdom." *SienceMag video*, 1:28, January 4, 2016. http://www.sciencemag.org/news/2016/01/video-chameleon-has-one-fastest-tongues-animal-kingdom
2. Jaacks, Jason. "Nature's Mood Rings: How Chameleons Really Change Color." *KQED Science video*, 3:38, August 25, 2015. https://ww2.kqed.org/science/2015/08/25/natures-mood-rings-how-chameleons-really-change-color/
3. Rosen, Bob. 2014. *Grounded: How Leaders Stay Rooted in an Uncertain World*. San Francisco: Jossey-Bass.
4. Eurich, Tasha. 2018. "What Self-Awareness Really Is (and How to Cultivate It)." *Harvard Business Review*, January 4, 2018. https://hbr.org/2018/01/what-self-awareness-really-is-and-how-to-cultivate-it
5. Harter, Jim. "Dismal Employee Engagement Is a Sign of Global Mismanagement." *Gallup News*, December 20, 2017. http://news.gallup.com/opinion/gallup/224012/dismal-employee-engagement-sign-global-mismanagement.aspx

Further Reading:

Friedman, Thomas L. 2016. *Thank You for Being Late: An Optimist's Guide to Thriving in the Age of Accelerations*. New York: Farrar, Straus and Giroux.

Mackinnon, Rebecca. 2017. "Trust Is Crumbling. Can Technology Help Restore It?" Review of *Who Can You Trust? How Technology Brought Us Together and Why It Might Drive Us Apart*, by Rachel Botsman, *Washington Post*, December 10, 2017. https://www.npr.org/2016/06/07/480976042/how-googles-laszlo-bock-is-making-work-better

Chapter 2: Conscious is the New Smart

1. *The Devil Wears Prada*. Directed by David Frankel. Twentieth Century Fox, 2006. DVD.
2. Rosen, Bob. 2017. *Leadership Journeys: Lessons from Global Leaders*. London: IEDP Developing Leaders. http://healthycompanies.com/wp-content/uploads/2017/10/Leadership-Journeys-eBook-Final-09-14-2017-1.pdf
3. Barra, Mary. "Written Testimony of General Motors Chief Executive Officer Mary Barra Before the House Committee on Energy and Commerce Subcommittee on Oversight and Investigations 'The GM Ignition Switch Recall: Why Did It Take So Long?'" Given at Congressional Hearing, April 1, 2014. Written testimony published March 31, 2014. http://media.gm.com/media/us/en/gm/news.detail.html/content/Pages/news/us/en/2014/mar/0331-barra-written-testimony.html
4. O'Brien, Michael J., and Larry Shook. 2010. *Quicksilver: A Revolutionary Way to Lead the Many and the Few – Beginning with You*. Spokane: The Printed Word, Inc.
5. Health, Thomas. 2018. "Meet the Carlyle Group's $174 Billion Man." *Washington Post*, February 4, 2018. https://www.washingtonpost.com/business/economy/meet-the-carlyle-groups-174-billion-man/2018/02/02/d47de690-06c3-11e8-8777-2a059f168dd2_story.html?utm_term=.128e03338f4a

Further Reading:

Anderson, Robert J., and William A. Adams. 2016. *Mastering Leadership: An Integrated Framework for Breakthrough Performance and Extraordinary Business Results*. Hoboken, NJ: Wiley.

Dethmer, Jim, Diana Chapman, and Kaley Warner Klemp. 2014. *The 15 Commitments of Conscious Leadership: A New Paradigm for Sustainable Success*. United States: Conscious Leadership Group.

Hess, Edward D., and Katherine Ludwig. 2017. *Humility Is the New Smart: Rethinking Human Excellence in the Smart Machine Age*. Oakland: Barrett-Koehler.

Koffman, Fred. 2006. *Conscious Business: How to Build Value Through Values.* Boulder, CO: Sounds True, Inc.

Palmer, Parker J. 1990. *The Active Life: A Spirituality of Work, Creativity, and Caring*. San Francisco, CA: Jossey-Bass.

Chapter 3: The Path to Being Conscious

1. "From Bike to Flight." Smithsonian National Air and Space Museum. Accessed December 15, 2017. https://airandspace.si.edu/exhibitions/wright-brothers/online/who/1895/biketoflight.cfm
2. Jun, Alex. "Inherent Instability: A Study of the F-16 Falcon." *Medium.com*, September 11, 2017. https://medium.com/@alexjun/interesting-aircraft-of-the-day-1-b8a64ed6fe57
3. *Merriam-Webster, s.v.* "Transformation." Accessed January 15, 2018. By permission. From Merriam-Webster.com © 2018 by Merriam-Webster, Inc. https://www.merriam-webster.com/dictionary/transformation
4. Surdey, Jessica. "Ask a Scientist: How Many Cells Are in a Person, and What Are the Kinds of Cells?" Binghamton University, accessed January 15, 2017. https://binghamton.edu/mpr/ask-a-scientist/entry.html?id=374
5. Sloman, Steven, and Philip Fernbach. 2017. *The Knowledge Illusion: Why We Never Think Alone.* New York: Riverhead Books.

Further Reading:

Mlodinow, Leonard. 2012. *Subliminal: How Your Unconscious Mind Rules Your Behavior*. New York: Random House.

Rosen, Bob. 2014. "Do You Shed Light or Cast Shadows?" *LinkedIn*, August 26, 2014. https://www.linkedin.com/pulse/20140826145703-22992958-do-you-shed-light-or-cast-shadows/

Rosen, Robert, with Paul B. Brown. 1996. *Leading People: Transforming Business from the Inside Out*. New York: The Penguin Group.

Chapter 4: Your Return on Investment

1. Verducci, Tom. 2017. *Cubs Way: The Zen of Building the Best Team in Baseball and Breaking the Curse.* New York: Penguin Random House.
2. Sheinin, Dave. 2017. "Smart Guys Win as Astros Ride Analytics to Championship." *Washington Post*, November 3, 2017, D4.
3. Sorkin, Andrew Ross. 2018. "BlackRock's Message: Contribute to Society, or Risk Losing Our Support." *New York Times*, January 15, 2018. https://www.nytimes.com/2018/01/15/business/dealbook/blackrock-laurence-fink-letter.html

Introduction to Go Deep

1. Drape, Joe. 2013. "Palace Malice, a Long Shot, Rewards a Promoter for His Patience." New York Times, June 8, 2013. http://www.nytimes.com/2013/06/09/sports/palace-malice-a-long-shot-wins-belmont-stakes.html

Chapter 5: Who is that Person in the Mirror?

1. Rosen, Bob. 2014. *Grounded: How Leaders Stay Rooted in an Uncertain World.* San Francisco: Jossey-Bass.
2. "An Overview of the Human Genome Project." National Human Genome Research Institute. Last updated May 11, 2016. https://www.genome.gov/12011238/an-overview-of-the-human-genome-project/
3. Rosen, *Grounded.*
4. Eurich, Tasha. 2018. "What Self-Awareness Really Is (and How to Cultivate It)." *Harvard Business Review,* January 4, 2018. https://hbr.org/2018/01/what-self-awareness-really-is-and-how-to-cultivate-it.
5. Ibid.

Further Reading:

Riso, Don Richard, and Russ Hudson. 1999. *The Wisdom of the Enneagram: The Complete Guide to Psychological and Spiritual Growth for the Nine Personality Types.* New York: Bantam Books.

Sierra, Hector, ed. 2014. "Your Personality Explained: Exploring the Science of Identity." *National Geographic,* Special Issue, 1–126.

Chapter 6: Discover your Innate Wisdom

1. Holiday, Ryan. 2012. "9 Lessons on Power and Leadership from Genghis Khan." *Forbes,* May 7, 2012. https://www.forbes.com/sites/ryanholiday/2012/05/07/9-lessons-on-leadership-from-genghis-khan-yes-genghis-khan/#69833cc56996
2. Trungpa, Chogyam. 2005. *The Sanity We Are Born With: A Buddhist Approach to Psychology.* Boston: Shambhala Publications, Inc.
3. Holiday, Ryan. 2012. "9 Lessons on Power and Leadership from Genghis Khan." *Forbes,* May 7, 2012. https://www.forbes.com/sites/ryanholiday/2012/05/07/9-lessons-on-leadership-from-genghis-khan-yes-genghis-khan/#69833cc56996
4. Rosen, Bob. 2014. *Grounded: How Leaders Stay Rooted in an Uncertain World.* San Francisco: Jossey-Bass.

Further Reading:

Kashdan, Todd B., and Robert Biswas-Diener. 2014. *The Upside of Your Dark Side: Why Being Your Whole Self-Not Just Your "Good" Self-Drives Success and Fulfillment*. New York: Penguin Group.

Levine, Noah. 2014. *Refuge Recovery: A Buddhist Path to Recovering from Addiction*. New York: HarperCollins.

Rosen, Bob. 2015. "Tough and Tender – The New Leadership." *A Grounded Leader Moment* December 15, 2015. http://bobrosen.com/2015/12/5053/

Rosen, Bob. 2016. "What's Love Got to Do with It?" *The Huffington Post*, February 9, 2016. https://www.huffingtonpost.com/bob-rosen/whats-love-got-to-do-with_11_b_9220904.html

Sharot, Tali. 2011. "The Optimism Bias." *Time Magazine*, June 6, 2011. 40–46.

Chapter 7: Can You See the Alligator in the Trees?

1. Dinets, Vladimir, Adam Britton, and Matthew Shirley. 2014. "Climbing Behavior in Extant Crocodilians." *Herpetology Notes*, Vol. 7, 3–7.
2. Hanson, Rick, and Richard Mendius, MD. 2009. *Buddha's Brain: The Practical Neuroscience of Happiness, Love, & Wisdom*. Oakland: New Harbinger Publications.
3. Rosen, Bob. 2017. *Leadership Journeys: Lessons from Global Leaders*. London: IEDP Developing Leaders. http://healthycompanies.com/wp-content/uploads/2017/10/Leadership-Journeys-eBook-Final-09-14-2017-1.pdf

Further Reading:

Rosen, Bob. 2014. "Hardwired to Hijack Yourself?" *LinkedIn*. August 19, 2014. https://www.linkedin.com/pulse/20140819150438-22992958-hardwired-to-hijack-yourself/

Chapter 8: Discomfort is the New Immunization

1. Madrigal, Alexis. 2013. "Someone Had to Invent Karaoke – This Guy Did." *The Atlantic*, December 18, 2013. https://www.theatlantic.com/technology/archive/2013/12/someone-had-to-invent-karaoke-this-guy-did/282491/
2. Hanson, Rick, and Richard Mendius. 2009. *Buddha's Brain: The Practical Neuroscience of Happiness, Love, & Wisdom*. Oakland: New Harbinger Publications.

3. McCoy, Terrence. 2014. "How Tourette's-Afflicted Tim Howard Went from International Ridicule to World Cup History." *The Washington Post,* July 2, 2014. https://www.washingtonpost.com/news/morning-mix/wp/2014/07/02/how-tourettes-afflicted-tim-howard-went-from-international-ridicule-to-world-cup-history/?utm_term=.97ed72c8285f
4. Kashdan, Todd B., and Robert Biswas-Diener. 2014. *The Upside of Your Dark Side: Why Being Your Whole Self-Not Just Your "Good" Self-Drives Success and Fulfillment.* New York: Penguin Group.

Further Reading:

Brown, Brené. 2012. *Daring Greatly: How the Courage to Be Vulnerable Transforms the Way We Live, Love, Parent, and Lead.* New York: Penguin Group.

Rosen, Bob. 2015. "The Power of Resilience." *LinkedIn Pulse*, January 21, 2015. https://www.linkedin.com/pulse/power-confidence-four-noble-truths-bob-rosen/

Chapter 9: Your Roots of Conscious Living

1. Jobs, Steve. "You've Got to Find What You Love." Commencement Speech, Stanford University Graduation, Stanford, June 12, 2005. Transcription published on June 14, 2005 https://news.stanford.edu/2005/06/14/jobs-061505/.
2. Rosen, Bob. 2014. *Grounded: How Leaders Stay Rooted in an Uncertain World.* San Francisco: Jossey-Bass.

Chapter 10: Travel Light

1. "Aviation Officials Remember September 11, 2001." *C-Span Video*, 1:45:18, September 11, 2010. https://www.c-span.org/video/?295417-1/aviation-officials-remember-september-11-2001
2. "Does Your Dog Resent You?" *Cesar's Way*, accessed January 17, 2017. https://www.cesarsway.com/dog-behavior/innocuous-behaviors/does-your-dog-resent-you
3. Lorenz, Peg. Interview by Healthy Companies. 2009.
4. Elkins, Kathleen. 2015. "From Poverty to a $3 Billion Fortune – The Incredible Rags-to-Riches Story of Oprah Winfrey." *Business Insider*, May 28, 2015, 1–4. http://www.businessinsider/com/rags-to-riches-story-of-oprah-winfrey-2015-5.

Further Reading:

David, Susan. 2016. *Emotional Agility: Get Unstuck, Embrace Change, and Thrive in Work and Life*. New York: Avery.

Gelles, David. 2016. "Mindfulness in Business: Is It Possible for Traditional Public Companies? Part 4 From a Series of Excerpts from David Gelles' Mindful Work." *B the Change*, May 17, 2016. https://bthechange.com/mindfulness-in-business-is-it-possible-for-traditional-public-companies-c76c49d99717

Seppala, Emma. 2015. "How Meditation Benefits CEOs." *Harvard Business Review*, December 14, 2015. https://hbr.org/2015/12/how-meditation-benefits-ceos

Wolever, Ruth Q., and Kyra J. Bobinet, Kelley McCabe, Elizabeth R. Mackenzie, Erin Fekete, Catherine A. Kusnick, and Michael Baime. 2012. "Effective and Viable Mind-Body Stress Reduction in the Workplace: A Randomized Controlled Trial." *Journal of Occupational Health Psychology*, Vol. 17, No. 2, 246–258.

Introduction of Think Big

1. "Jimmy Wales." *Wikipedia*, last modified January 3, 2018, https://en.wikiquote.org/wiki/Jimmy_Wales#C-SPAN_interview_(2005)
2. Rosen, Bob. 2017. *Leadership Journeys: Lessons from Global Leaders*. London: IEDP Developing Leaders. http://healthycompanies.com/wp-content/uploads/2017/10/Leadership-Journeys-eBook-Final-09-14-2017-1.pdf

Further Reading:

Lee, Jaclyn. 2017. "5 Crucial Skills For The New Digital Economy." *Avvanz*, January 03, 2017. https://www.avvanz.com/blog/5-key-skills-needed-in-the-digital-economy/

Chapter 11: A 280-Character Universe

1. Castillo, Michelle. 2017. "Reed Hastings' Story About the Founding of Netflix has Changed Several Times." *CNBC Tech*, May 23, 2017. https://www.cnbc.com/2017/05/23/netflix-ceo-reed-hastings-on-how-the-company-was-born.html
2. Ibid.
3. Mlodinow, Leonard. 2012. *Subliminal: How Your Unconscious Mind Rules Your Behavior*. New York: Random House.

4. Carr, Nicholas. 2011. *The Shallows: What the Internet is Doing to Our Brains.* New York: W. W. Norton & Company.

Further Reading:

Rosen, Robert. 2008. *Just Enough Anxiety: The Hidden Driver of Business Success.* New York: The Penguin Group.

Rosen, Robert. 2015. "Confronting Reality." *LinkedIn Pulse*, February 3, 2015. https://www.linkedin.com/pulse/confronting-reality-bob-rosen/

Rosen, Bob. 2017. *Leadership Journeys: Lessons from Global Leaders.* London: IEDP Developing Leaders. http://healthycompanies.com/wp-content/uploads/2017/10/Leadership-Journeys-eBook-Final-09-14-2017-1.pdf

Chapter 12: Be Your Own Drone

1. Peters, Adele. 2017. "Filled with Blood and Drugs, These Delivery Drones Are Saving Lives in Africa." *Fast Company*, August 24, 2017, https://www.fastcompany.com/40457183/filled-with-blood-and-medical-supplies-these-delivery-drones-are-saving-lives-in-africa
2. Keillor, Garrison. 2016. "*A Prairie Home Companion.*" National Public Radio. 1974–2016.
3. Eurich, Tasha. 2018. "What Self-Awareness Really Is (and How to Cultivate It)." *Harvard Business Review*, January 4, 2018. https://hbr.org/2018/01/what-self-awareness-really-is-and-how-to-cultivate-it.

Chapter 13: Leverage your Personal Ecosystem

1. Murthy, Viveck. 2017. "Work and the Loneliness Epidemic." *Harvard Business Review*, September 27, 2017. https://www.vivekmurthy.com/single-post/2017/10/10/Work-and-the-Loneliness-Epidemic-Harvard-Business-Review
2. Fulghum, Robert. 2003. *All I Ever Needed to Know I Learned in Kindergarten: Reconsidered, Revised & Expanded with Twenty-Five New Essays.* New York: Ballantine Books.
3. Arena, Michael. Interview by Healthy Companies. 2017.

Further Reading:

Brown, Brené. 2017. *Braving the Wilderness: The Quest for True Belonging and the Courage to Stand Alone.* New York: Random House.

Cross, Bob, Reb Rebele, and Adam Grant. 2016. "Collaborative Overload." *Harvard Business Review*, January February 2016 Issue, 74–79.

Rosen, Bob. 2014. *Grounded: How Leaders Stay Rooted in an Uncertain World.* San Francisco: Jossey-Bass.

Chapter 14: Develop Your Google Mind

1. D'Monte, Leslie and Zahra Khan. 2013. "I Just Happen to Be a Woman Who Is Aggressive: Ruchi Sanghvi." *Livemint.com*, November 30, 2013. http://www.livemint.com/Companies/XmqafmHKXq3U45sB3LdsYL/I-just-happen-to-be-a-woman-who-is-aggressive-Ruchi-Sanghvi.html
2. Brown, Tim. 2017. "How I Made the Switch to AI Research." *South Park Commons*, August 3, 2017. https://medium.com/south-park-commons/how-i-made-the-switch-to-ai-research-b053b402608
3. Wu, Sandra. 2016. "The Reading Habits of Highly Successful People." *Brinklist Magazine*, December 22, 2016. https://www.blinkist.com/magazine/posts/reading-habits-of-highly-successful-people
4. Dweck, Carol S. 2008. *Mindset: The New Psychology of Success*. New York: Ballantine Books.
5. Vedantam, Shankar. "How Google's Laszlo Bock Is Making Work Better." *Hidden Brain*, NPR, June 7, 2016. https://www.npr.org/2016/06/07/480976042/how-googles-laszlo-bock-is-making-work-better

Further Reading:

Liedtka, Jeanne, Robert Rosen, and Robert Wiltbank. 2009. *The Catalyst: How YOU Can Become an Extraordinary Growth Leader*. New York: Crown Business.

Rosen, Bob. 2015. "Do You Have a Growth Mindset?" *A Grounded Leader Moment*, September 11, 2015. http://bobrosen.com/2015/09/growth-mindset/

Chapter 15: "And" is the new "Or"

1. Hitti, Miranda. "Viagra May Help Severe Altitude Sickness." *WebMD*, 2005, https://www.webmd.com/men/news/20050201/viagra-may-help-severe-altitude-sickness#2
2. Rosen, Bob. 2017. *Leadership Journeys: Lessons from Global Leaders*. London: IEDP Developing Leaders. http://healthycompanies.com/wp-content/uploads/2017/10/Leadership-Journeys-eBook-Final-09-14-2017-1.pdf

Further Reading:

Rosen, Bob. 2014. "How Leaders Can Get Comfortable with Paradoxes." *Linked in*. October 7, 2014. https://www.linkedin.com/pulse/20141007213943-22992958-how-leaders-can-get-comfortable-with-paradoxes/

Schroeder-Saulnier, Deborah. 2014. *The Power of Paradox: Harness the Energy of Competing Ideas to Uncover Radically Innovative Solutions.* Pompton Plains: Career Press.

Smith, Wendy K., Marianne W. Lewis, and Michael Tushman. 2016. "'Both/And' Leadership." *Harvard Business Review*, May 2016 Issue. https://hbr.org/2016/05/both-and-leadership.

Chapter 16: Inclusion is the Road to Innovation

1. Denselow, Robin. 2012. "Paul Simon's Graceland: The Acclaim and the Outrage." *Vimeo*, April 19, 2012. https://www.theguardian.com/music/2012/apr/19/paul-simon-graceland-acclaim-outrage
2. Wikipedia. 2018. "List of Cognitive Biases." Last modified January 19, 2018. https://en.wikipedia.org/wiki/List_of_cognitive_biases
3. Schwab, Katherine. 2017. "IDEO Studied Innovation in 100+ Companies – Here's What It Found." *CO.DESIGN*, March 20, 2017. https://www.fastcodesign.com/3069069/ideo-studied-innovation-in-100-companies-heres-what-it-found
4. Arlington County. 2017. "County Vision." https://departments.arlingtonva.us/cmo/county-vision/
5. Niche. 2016. "Best Cities to Live in America." Niche.com, Inc. https://www.niche.com/places-to-live/search/best-cities/

Further Reading

Arlington County. 2017. "County Awards and Recognition." Awards by Topic. https://departments.arlingtonva.us/cmo/county-awards-recognition/

InsideNOVA. 2016. "Uniquely Arlington: 'The Arlington Way' Remains Elusive to Define." *InsideNOVA*, October 5, 2016. http://www.insidenova.com/news/arlington/uniquely-arlington-the-arlington-way-remains-elusive-to-define/article_0bf65318-6b4f-11e5-bffd-7b81d88da822.html#comments

Liedtka, Jeanne M., and Randy Salzman. 2017. "Designing for Growth: 5 Keys to Innovation" *Darden Ideas To Action*, April 10, 2017. https://ideas.darden.virginia.edu/2017/04/designing-for-growth-5-keys-to-innovation/

Lockwood, Nancy R. 2016. "Workplace Diversity: Leveraging the Power of Difference for Competitive Advantage." *Jobs in Chicago*, July 20, 2016. http://jobchicago.net/workplace-diversity-leveraging-the-power-of-difference-for-competitive-advantage/

Porter, Jane. 2014. "You're More Biased Than You Think." *Fast Company*, October 6, 2014, 3–5. https://www.fastcompany.com/3036627/youre-more-biased-than-you-think

Rosen, Robert. 2014. "Celebrate Cultural Diversity as An Asset" *LinkedIn Pulse*, September 23, 2014. https://www.linkedin.com/pulse/20140923151116-22992958-celebrate-cutural-diversity-as-an-asset/

Rosen, Robert, Patricia Digh, Marshall Singer, and Carl Phillips. 2000. *Global Literacies: Lessons on Business Leadership and National Cultures*. New York: Simon & Schuster.

Vedantam, Shankar. 2017. "How Silicon Valley Can Help You Get Unstuck." *Hidden Brain*, NPR, January 3, 2017. https://www.npr.org/2017/01/03/507901716/how-silicon-valley-can-help-you-get-unstuck

Introduction to Get Real

1. Dodds, Colin. 2017. "Elon Musk Biography." *Investopedia*. December 27, 2017. https://www.investopedia.com/university/elon-musk-biography/
2. "Elon Musk Biography: Success Story of the 21st Century Innovator." *Astrum People*, accessed December 30, 2017. https://astrumpeople.com/elon-musk-biography/
3. Hess, Abigail. 2017. "How Tesla and Elon Musk Became Household Names." *CNBC Make It*, November 21, 2017. https://www.cnbc.com/2017/11/21/how-tesla-and-elon-musk-became-household-names.html
4. Dodds, "Elon Musk Biography."

Further Reading:

Hess, Edward D., and Katherine Ludwig. 2017. *Humility Is the New Smart: Rethinking Human Excellence in the Smart Machine Age*. Oakland: Barrett-Koehler.

Chapter 17: Transforming Yourself

1. Rosen, Robert, with Paul B. Brown. 1996. *Leading People: Transforming Business from the Inside Out*. New York: The Penguin Group.
2. Shepard, Judy. 2009. *The Meaning of Matthew: My Son's Murder in Laramie, and a World Transformed*. New York: Penguin Group.
3. Shepard, Judy. Interview by Healthy Companies. 2017.

Further Reading:

Anderson, Robert J. and William A. Adams. 2016. *Mastering Leadership: An Integrated Framework for Breakthrough Performance and Extraordinary Business Results*. Hoboken: John Wiley & Sons.

Berger, Jennifer Garvey. 2012. *Changing on the Job: Developing Leaders for a Complex World*. Stanford: Stanford Business Books.

Chapter 18: Three Faces of Anxiety

1. Rosen, Robert. 2008. *Just Enough Anxiety: The Hidden Driver of Business Success.* New York: The Penguin Group.
2. Madgett, Mark. 2017. "Opening Remarks." Speech. New York Life 2017 Agency Town Hall.

Further Reading:

Rosen, Robert. 2008. "Just Enough Anxiety" *Training Journal*, April 2008:33–36. www.trainingjournal.com

"Mark Madgett Bio." *New York Life*, June 25, 2015. https://www.newyorklife.com/newsroom/executive-biographies/mark-madgett-bio/

Chapter 19: Feeding Your Accelerators

1. Gent, Edd. 2017. "The Unsurpassed 125-Year-Old Network that Feeds Mumbai." *BBC FutureNow*, January 16, 2017. http://www.bbc.com/future/story/20170114-the-125-year-old-network-that-keeps-mumbai-going
2. Smith, Tammy. Interview by Healthy Companies. 2017.
3. Ericsson, K. A., R. T. Krampe, and C. Tesch-Römer. 1993. "The Role of Deliberate Practice in the Acquisition of Expert Performance." *Psychological Review*, Vol. 100, No. 3, 363–406.

Further Reading:

"About Us." Dabbawala site, accessed January 11, 2017. http://mumbaidabbawala.in

"DabbaWalas – Amazing Meal Delivery in India." YouTube video, 3:55, posted by "geobeats," November 4, 2009. https://www.youtube.com/watch?v=fTkGDXRnR9I

David, Susan. 2016. *Emotional Agility: Get Unstuck, Embrace Change, and Thrive in Work and Life*. New York: Avery.

Hess, Edward D., and Katherine Ludwig. 2017. *Humility Is the New Smart: Rethinking Human Excellence in the Smart Machine Age*. Oakland: Barrett-Koehler.

Somaskanda, Sumi, and Mandakini Gahlot. 2014. "This Indian Meal Service Is So Efficient It's the Envy of FedEx." *PRI Business, Economics, and Jobs*, July 15, 2014. https://www.pri.org/stories/2014-07-15/indian-meal-service-so-efficient-it-s-envy-fedex

Swann, Emma-Kate. 2017. "Grounded and Conscious Leadership." Workshop, Transformational Leadership Series, Healthy Companies International.

Chapter 20: Befriend Your Hijackers

1. Crouse, Karen. 2016. "Seeking Answers, Michael Phelps Finds Himself." *New York Times*, June 24, 2016. https://www.nytimes.com/2016/06/26/sports/olympics/michael-phelps-swimming-rehab.html
2. Drehs, Wayne. 2016. "Michael Phelps' Final Turn." *ESPN the Magazine*, June 23, 2016. http://www.espn.com/espn/feature/story/_/id/16425548/michael-phelps-prepares-life-2016-rio-olympics
3. Crouse, "Seeking Answers."
4. Layden, Tim. 2015. "After Rehabilitation, the Best of Michael Phelps May Lie Ahead." *Sports Illustrated*, November 9, 2015. https://www.si.com/olympics/2015/11/09/michael-phelps-rehabilitation-rio-2016
5. Crouse, "Seeking Answers."
6. Ibid.
7. Ibid.
8. Drehs. "Michael Phelps' Final Turn."
9. Harter, Jim. "Dismal Employee Engagement Is a Sign of Global Mismanagement." *Gallup News*. December 20, 2017. http://news.gallup.com/opinion/gallup/224012/dismal-employee-engagement-sign-global-mismanagement.aspx

Further Reading:

Crouse, Karen. 2016. "Seeking Answers, Michael Phelps Finds Himself." *New York Times*, June 24, 2016. https://www.nytimes.com/2016/06/26/sports/olympics/michael-phelps-swimming-rehab.html

Crouse, Karen. 2017. "Michael Phelps Enjoys Victory Lap with Jordan Spieth at Pro-Am." *The New York Times*, February 1, 2017. https://www.nytimes.com/2017/02/01/sports/michael-phelps-enjoys-victory-lap-with-jordan-spieth-at-pro-am.html

David, Susan. 2016. *Emotional Agility: Get Unstuck, Embrace Change, and Thrive in Work and Life*. New York: Avery.

Drehs, Wayne. 2016. "Michael Phelps Final Turn." *ESPN the Magazine*, June 23, 2016. http://www.espn.com/espn/feature/story/_/id/16425548/michael-phelps-prepares-life-2016-rio-olympics

Goldsmith, Marshall, and Mark Reiter. 2015. *Triggers: Creating Behavior That Lasts – Becoming the Person You Want to Be*. New York: Crown Business.

Majendie, Matt. 2016. "Michael Phelps: How Swimming Legend Regained His Immortality.'" *CNN*, August 14, 2016. http://www.cnn.com/2016/08/13/sport/michael-phelps-legacy-rio-2016-olympics/index.html

Swann, Emma-Kate. 2017. "Grounded and Conscious Leadership." Workshop, Transformational Leadership Series, Healthy Companies International.

Introduction to Step Up

1. Smith, Chris. 2012. "The Mayor in the Eye." *New York News & Politics*, November 11, 2012. http://nymag.com/news/features/bloomberg-hurricane-sandy-2012-11/
2. Carrington, Damian. 2017. "Michael Bloomberg's 'War on Coal' Goes Global with $50m Fund." *The Guardian*, November 9, 2017. https://www.theguardian.com/environment/2017/nov/09/michael-bloombergs-war-on-coal-goes-global-with-50m-fund
3. Rahim, Saqib. 2012. "Climate Change Influence on Superstorm Sandy Drives Bloomberg to Endorse Obama." *Scientific American ClimateWire*, November 2, 2012. https://www.scientificamerican.com/article/climate-change-influence-superstorm-sandy-drives-bloomberg-endorse-obama/

Chapter 21: Live Your Higher Purpose

1. Arena, Christine. 2007. *The High-Purpose Company: The Truly Responsible - and Highly Profitable - Firms That Are Changing Business Now*. New York: HarperCollins.
2. Rosen, Bob. 2015. "The Seduction of Power." *LinkedIn Pulse*, March 2, 2015. https://www.linkedin.com/pulse/fifty-shades-power-bob-rosen/?trk=mp-reader-card
3. Rosen, Bob. 2014. "For Pete Frates, It's About the Cause, Not the Ice Bucket." *The Healthy Leader*, August 22, 2014. https://healthycompanies.com/ice-bucket-challenge/

Further Reading:

Anderson, Robert J., and William A. Adams. 2016. *Mastering Leadership: An Integrated Framework for Breakthrough Performance and Extraordinary Business Results*. Hoboken, NJ: Wiley.

Baltzley, Dennis, and Jeff Lawrence. 2016. "Candor and Transparency in the Service of Purpose." *People + Strategy*, Vol. 39, No. 4, 21–25.

Pfieffer, Jeffrey. 2016. "Tell Me Lies, Tell Me Sweet Little Lies: The Many Positive Functions of Being Untruthful." *People + Strategy*, Vol. 39, No. 4, 32–35.

Chapter 22: Amplify your Personal Sensors

1. Boykin, Jennifer. Interview by Healthy Companies. 2017.
2. Ceballos, Lucas. Interview by Healthy Companies. 2017.

Chapter 23: Lead With Constructive Impatience

1. Rosen, Bob. 2017. *Leadership Journeys: Lessons from Global Leaders*. London: IEDP Developing Leaders. http://healthycompanies.com/wp-content/uploads/2017/10/Leadership-Journeys-eBook-Final-09-14-2017-1.pdf
2. Bezos, Jeff. 2016. "2016 Letter to Shareholders." April 12, 2017. https://www.amazon.com/p/feature/z6o9g6sysxur57t
3. "Relentless.com." 2014. *The Economist*, June 19, 2014. https://www.economist.com/news/briefing/21604559-20-amazon-bulking-up-it-notyetslowing-down-relentlesscom

Further Reading:

Rosen, Robert. 2008. *Just Enough Anxiety: The Hidden Driver of Business Success*. New York: The Penguin Group.

Rosen, Robert. 2008. "Mastering the Emotional Side of Change." *Chief Learning Officer*, November 2008. http://www.clomedia.com/2008/10/27/mastering-the-emotional-side-of-change/

Chapter 24: Make Civility Your Guide

1. Shandwick, Weber, and Powell Tate. 2010. "Civility in America: An Annual Nationwide Survey." WeberShandwick.com Newsroom. http://www.webershandwick.com/news/article/civility
2. Wong, Edward. 2001. "A Stinging Office Memo Boomerangs; Chief Executive is Criticized After Upbraiding Workers by Email." *New York*

Times, April 5, 2001. http://www.nytimes.com/2001/04/05/business/stinging-office-memo-boomerangs-chief-executive-criticized-after-upbraiding.html

3. Gensheimer, Mark. Interview by Healthy Companies. 2017.
4. Bersin & Associates. 2001. "New Bersin & Associates Research Shows Organizations That Excel at Employee Recognition Are 12 Times More Likely to Generate Strong Business Results." http://www.bersin.com/News/Content.aspx?id=16023

Further Reading:

Brody, Jane. "Forging Social Connections for Longer Life." *New York Times*, March 26, 2012. http://well.blogs.nytimes.com/2012/03/26/forging-social-connections-for-longer-life

Porath, Christine. 2017. "How Rudeness Stops People from Working Together." *Harvard Business Review*, January 20, 2017. https://hbr.org/2017/01/how-rudeness-stops-people-from-working-together

Chapter 25: Build a Shared Consciousness

1. Friedman, Thomas L. 2016. *Thank You for Being Late: An Optimist's Guide to Thriving in the Age of Accelerations*. New York: Farrar, Straus and Giroux.
2. Brown, Brené. 2017. *Braving the Wilderness: The Quest for True Belonging and the Courage to Stand Alone.* New York: Random House.
3. Hernandez, Grissel. Interview by Healthy Companies. 2017.
4. Rosen, Bob. 2017. *Leadership Journeys: Lessons from Global Leaders.* London: IEDP Developing Leaders. http://healthycompanies.com/wp-content/uploads/2017/10/Leadership-Journeys-eBook-Final-09-14-2017-1.pdf
5. Friedman, *Thank You for Being Late.*
6. Brody, Jane. "Forging Social Connections for Longer Life." *New York Times*, March 26, 2012. http://well.blogs.nytimes.com/2012/03/26/forging-social-connections-for-longer-life
7. Ibid.
8. Friedman, *Thank You for Being Late.*

Further Reading:

McChrystal, Stanley with Tantum Collins, David Silverman, and Chris Fussell. 2015. *Team of Teams: New Rules of Engagement for a Complex World*. New York: Penguin Publishing Group.

Chapter 26: Help your Garden Grow

1. Stout, Soma. Interview by Healthy Companies. 2017.
2. Rosen, Bob. 2014. *Grounded: How Leaders Stay Rooted in an Uncertain World*. San Francisco: Jossey-Bass.
3. Handy, Charles. 2001. *The Elephant and the Flea: Reflections of a Reluctant Capitalist*. Boston: Harvard Business School Press.
4. Garten, Eric and Michael Mankins. 2015. "Engaging Your Employees Is Good, but Don't Stop There." *Harvard Business Review*, December 9, 2015. https://hbr.org/2015/12/engaging-your-employees-is-good-but-dont-stop-there

Further Reading:

Peterson, Tom. 2016. "Transforming Health Through Community Partnership." *Stakeholder Health, Q & A: Soma Stout of 100 Million Healthier Lives*, June 8, 2016. https://stakeholderhealth.org/soma-stout/

Chapter 27: Leave a Legacy

1. Nodjimbadem, Katie. 2015. "The 390-Year-Old Tree That Survived the Bombing of Hiroshima." *Smithsonian.com*, August 4, 2015. https://www.smithsonianmag.com/history/390-year-old-tree-survived-bombing-hiroshima-180956157/
2. Siddiqui, Faiz. 2015. "This 390-Year-Old Bonsai Tree Survived an Atomic Bomb and No One Knew Until 2001." *Washington Post*, August 2, 2015. https://www.washingtonpost.com/local/the-390-year-old-tree-that-survived-an-atomic-bomb/2015/08/02/3f824dae-3945-11e5-8e98-115a3cf7d7ae_story.html?utm_term=.d118c0b0ed59

Further Reading:

"400-Year-Old Bonsai Survived Hiroshima Bombing." YouTube video, 4:32, August 3, 2010. https://www.youtube.com/watch?v=NYPeNcnyZ6g&feature=youtu.be

Acknowledgments

Bob Rosen

To Jay, who brings love into my life every day and teaches me about the power of staying conscious at home and in far-off places around the world.

To Emma-Kate for her powerful mind, exuberant energy, and deep commitment to living the principles of this book. You are making a special mark on the world every day.

To Nancy Dailey for her amazing intellect, brilliant creativity, and exquisite writing skills, who has helped bring this book alive.

To my family, who help me stay conscious. Thanks for all your love and support, Jay Fisette; Barbara and Richard Keast; Randi, Danny, Ryan, Lauren, Chris, Sarah, Devon, Lucas, and McKenna Tancini; Margot Fisette; Lynne and Mark Salvaggio; Paul, Nancy, Kyle, and Melanie Fisette: Erin, Mac, Molly, Harper, and Hudson McGinn; Amanda Salvaggio, Curtis George, Charlie, and Jane; and Michael and Jack Salvaggio.

To our colleagues at Healthy Companies who inspire and challenge us every day: Jim Mathews, Rick Auman, David Knauss, John Bocko, Joe Trueblood, Susan Smith, Brandy Freeman, Grace Groover, and Lysandra Mandry, and the many coaches and consultants we work with around the world. Thanks to our advisors Tony Buzzelli, Mitch Kosh, Barry Schub, Tom Waldron, and Kathie Ross for championing our work. To our colleagues at Renner and Odato who keep us grounded and visible in the world. Our lives would not be the same without you.

Thanks to my dear friends who live many of the principles in this book and have always supported me and my work: Berard Tierney, Patrick Leonard, Jeff Akman, Bob Witeck, Mark Treadaway, Bob Kenney, Lance Wolf, Pedro Nunez, Dan Pikos, Carol Rickard, Scott Brideau, Glenn and Carol Davidson, Jonathan Peck, Carlos Berio, Sam Paschall, Jon Sade, David Mills, and Adam Connerton. To my other friends who brighten my life and make the world a better place.

To my dear friend and agent Gail Ross, and Howard Yoon, for believing in me and my voice over many years. To all our friends at Wiley, who continue to lead the world of publishing great books. And to Mark Fortier, who helps us let the world know about our important work.

To the thousands of leadership thinkers and writers who continue to shine light on the field of study. Finally, to the thousands of executives and managers who live these principles every day.

Emma-Kate Swann

To Peter, who teaches me the power of conscious leadership every day at home, with friends, family, students, and parents to build healthy communities.

To my parents, Robin and Kaye, who are the best role models of conscious leadership I could ever have hoped for.

To Bob, for your huge heart full of love, and for encouraging and believing in me to step up into new possibilities to reach my full potential. I am grateful for every day I have with you to learn, grow, and share the journey in building conscious communities of leaders around the globe. What a gift!

To my colleagues at Healthy Companies, who inspire and challenge me every day.

To my family, who have loved and supported me unconditionally through this journey: Peter Kenah, Nicole Kenah, Erin Kenah, Robin Swann, Kaye Swann, Troy Swann, Annette Swann, Phoenix Swann, Amelie Swann, Isaac Swann, Ro Boersma, Ana Kenah, Venecia Rojas, Bill Kenah, Megan Kenah, Nate Hirsch, Amy Gleklen, Jon Gleklen, Luke Coghlan, Amy Coghlan, and Faye Millard.

To my dearest friends Emily MacMahon, Alejandra Duran-Bohme, and Amy Gleklen for always believing in me and helping me grow over the years as we continue to share the lifelong journey of conscious leadership.

About the Authors

Bob Rosen, PhD, is a trusted CEO adviser, organizational psychologist, and best-selling author. He has long been on a mission to transform the world of business, one leader at a time. Bob founded Healthy Companies International 30 years ago with the singular goal of helping executives achieve their leadership potential. With support from a multiyear grant from the John D. and Catherine T. MacArthur Foundation, Bob and his colleagues began an in-depth study of leadership. Since then, he has personally interviewed more than five hundred CEOs—in 55 countries—in organizations as diverse as Ford, Motorola, Johnson & Johnson, Singapore Airlines, Brinks, Northrop Grumman, Toyota, Citigroup, PepsiCo, ING, and PricewaterhouseCoopers. He has become an adviser to many of these companies.

Bob is a frequent global keynote speaker and sought-after advisor to boards, CEOs, and executive teams around the world. He has spoken on issues ranging from leading transformation and leading people to leading growth and leading globally. The underlying foundation of all his work is the power of being a grounded and conscious leader as the catalyst for personal and organizational success. Clients include Global 2000 corporations, government and nongovernmental organizations, and selected associations around the world.

Bob is a frequent media commentator who has been quoted in the *New York Times, Wall Street Journal, Fortune, Bloomberg Businessweek, Financial Times, Time, Chief Executive Magazine,* and more. Bob's books include *The Healthy Company, Leading People, Just Enough Anxiety, Global Literacies, The Catalyst,* and the *New York Times* best seller *Grounded.* Bob graduated from the University of Virginia. He subsequently earned a PhD in clinical psychology at the University of Pittsburgh. Bob teaches in executive education programs and has been a longtime faculty member in the Department of Psychiatry and Behavioral Sciences at George Washington University's School of Medicine.

For more information, please visit BobRosen.com and healthycompanies.com.

Emma-Kate Swann is an organizational psychologist and executive coach. She has been working in the areas of organizational development, executive coaching, organizational change and transformation, and leadership development for the past 20 years. She is currently the vice president of leadership and transformation at Healthy Companies International. Emma-Kate's mission is to build communities of conscious leaders to maximize their performance and create sustainable, healthy organizational cultures. As part of this mission, Emma-Kate coaches executives on optimizing their performance, helps organizations navigate through change, and guides executive teams in building more productive relationships. She is also responsible for the product development of Healthy Companies' Grounded and Conscious Learning Solutions.

Prior to joining Healthy Companies, Emma-Kate served in a variety of senior leadership roles at PricewaterhouseCoopers and CEB. She is asked to speak regularly on a wide range of topics, including effective executive coaching; creating and sustaining healthy, high-performing cultures; and cultivating key talent. With extensive experience living and working in Australia, New Zealand, central and western Europe, Asia, Africa, and North America, Emma-Kate brings a uniquely informed and global perspective to her work.

Emma-Kate holds a master's in organizational psychology from the University of New South Wales and a BA honours in psychology from Macquarie University in Sydney, Australia. She is also an ICF-accredited executive coach (PCC) through Georgetown University in Washington, DC. Emma-Kate is passionate about integrating health and wellness with the psychology of behavior change; she is a certified yoga instructor and eating psychology coach, and enjoys spending time with her husband, Peter, and two stepdaughters, Nicole and Erin.

Index

Page references followed by *fig* indicate an illustrated figure.

O

P

A SPECIAL OFFER

Bring Bob and His Message to Your Organization

- Sought-after keynote speaker
- *New York Times* bestselling author
- Founder of Healthy Companies
- Top CEO adviser

Bob Rosen is a trusted CEO adviser, organizational psychologist, and best-selling author. As one of the more influential leadership thinkers in the world today, Bob uses the power of storytelling, as well as interactive visuals and tools, to illustrate his leadership insights for audiences around the globe.

The underlying foundation of all his work is the power of being a grounded and conscious leader, and building high-performance executive teams as the catalyst for personal and organizational success.

As a frequent keynote speaker, Bob challenges audience members to better understand and transform themselves as leaders, to explore the essential dimensions of grounded leadership and to leverage their own personal and organizational accelerators and hijackers to produce world-class outcomes.

A sought-after media commentator who has appeared in the *New York Times, Wall Street Journal, Fortune, Bloomberg Businessweek, Financial Times,* and *Time,* Bob's books include *The Healthy Company, Leading People, Just Enough Anxiety, Global Literacies, The Catalyst,* and the *New York Times* best seller *Grounded: How Leaders Stay Rooted in an Uncertain World.*

For more information, please call (703) 351–9901 or visit **healthycompanies.com**.